IVAN AGUÉLI
SENSATION OF ETERNITY
Selected Writings

For information, email:
info@ivanagueli.com

ISBN: 978-91-519-8509-1

Ivan Aguéli

SENSATION
OF ETERNITY

Selected Writings

Translated & Edited by
Oliver Fotros

بسم الله الرحمن الرحيم

[Ivan Aguéli's handwriting]

Abdul Hâdî

Ivan Aguéli around 1903-1905 in Cairo.
Photographer unknown.

*"Regrettably, I must prevail.
I am condemned to live on,
for my art shall one day explain
the eccentricities of my life.*

*I am the slave of a tradition
I cannot deny."*

Abdul Hâdi

Contents

FOREWORD

WELL OVER A CENTURY HAS PASSED since his death in 1917, yet Ivan Aguéli remains strangely unknown outside his home country of Sweden. Aguéli, or *Shaykh Abdul Hâdi Aqhîli,* was an artist and anarchist who converted to Islam in 1898, studied at *al Azhar,* and then devoted his life to the universalist Sufi teachings of Muhyeddin Ibn Arabi.

Abdul Hâdi was not only a "chronological" pioneer in the introduction of Sufism in the West, but he was also a scholar of immense erudition and insight. I am certain that many readers of his works will agree with me that Abdul Hâdi should undoubtedly be recognised as one of the great luminaries of 20th Century Islam.

I am therefore pleased to for the first time present a well overdue English anthology of Abdul Hâdi's works. I sincerely hope that the readers of this book will not only benefit from the wisdom it contains, but also be inspired to grant him the recognition he deserves.

Oliver Fotros

BIOGRAPHY

by Oliver Fotros

JOHN GUSTAF AGELII, OR "IVAN AGUÉLI", was born in 1869 in the Swedish town of Sala. The son of the town veterinarian, he was from an early age sent to a boarding school in Stockholm where he, through a friend, was introduced to the teachings of the 18th Century Swedish mystic Emanuel Swedenborg. It was most probably through his studies of Swedenborg – to whom he also was related through his mother – that Aguéli first discovered the teachings of Islam. A gifted painter, Aguéli moved to Paris in the early 1890s, where he learnt to know the Symbolist painter Émile Bernard and was drawn into anarchist circles. As an anarchist, he was in 1894 tried and acquitted in the "Trial of the Thirty". Although the exact circumstances of his conversion to Islam are not known, it occurred in Paris sometime during the year 1898, after which Aguéli often referred to himself by the name of "*Abdul Hâdi*".

In 1899, Aguéli travelled to Ceylon, where he lived for a short while amongst the Muslims of Colombo. It was there that he learnt to know the Sufi entourage of the exiled Egyptian Ahmed Urabi, who was a good friend of Abd ar-Rahman Elish, a renowned Sufi Shaykh living in Cairo. When Aguéli subsequently moved to Cairo in late 1902, he approached Shaykh Elish who initiated him into the Shadiliyyah order. Enrolling at *Al Azhar*, Aguéli furthered his studies in Islam and Arabic whilst also co-founding an Italian-Arabic periodical called "*Il Convito*". Met with hostility from the British Administration and Muslim fundamentalists, Il Convito braved on until its closure in 1908. By now, Aguéli had become a "*muqaddim*" ("representative") of Shaykh Elish and returned to Europe in 1909 to teach the universalist doctrines of Sufism.

Having first settled in Geneva, Aguéli returned to Paris in early 1910 where he published articles in the esoteric periodical *La Gnose*. Becoming a good friend of the editor, a young man by the name of René Guénon, Aguéli proceeded to on 22 June 1911 initiate him into Sufism, giving him the name "Abdul Wahid". He also founded the "Al Akbariyyah", an esoteric society devoted to the teachings of the Sufi Muhyeddin Ibn Arabi.

Leaving Paris, a mere week after the initiation of Guénon, Aguéli stayed for a year in Sweden, until he returned to France in mid-1912. After a year of roaming the French countryside, he returned to Egypt in late 1913, where he stayed until the outbreak of the First World War. In 1916, weary of pro-Ottoman agitators, the British Administration ordered his deportation to Spain on the rather vague charges of wearing "Bedouin clothing" and only mixing with Arabs.

Lacking funds to return to Sweden, Aguéli was subsequently trapped in Catalonia, where he lived a life of great hardship until he, in late 1917, tragically perished in a presumed train accident in the outskirts of Barcelona.

*Ivan Aguéli (Abdul Hâdi) in late 1880s
in Sweden. Photographer: A. Wallin.*

"Presume for an instant, that all copies of the Sublime Scripture were destroyed, and every believer was slain to the very last man:
        Islam would still live on, for its abode is not of this world."

L'Initiation

1902

INTRODUCTION

"Notes sur L'Islam" was the very first article Ivan Aguéli published on the topic of Islam. It was written in 1902, two years after his return from his travels in South Asia. It was published in "L'Initiation", the periodical of the Martinist Order, which was edited by Leon Champrenaud.

Having converted to Islam in 1898 in Paris, Aguéli's first contact with a Muslim community was in Ceylon in 1899. The experience of living in Colombo's diverse Muslim community – amongst Malays, Arabs, Persians, Afghans and Indians – is clearly seen in his observation of what he calls Islam's "synthetic" and "emancipatory" power.

The article also touches upon topics that were later reiterated by René Guénon, such as "East" and "West", the death of the Templars as the beginning of darker times, and the misdeeds of Christian missionaries.

There are also traces of Aguéli's left-wing leanings, by which he saw Western anarchism as being necessary to right the wrongs done by modernism to the downtrodden masses of Europe. Regarding Aguéli's "anarchism", it should nevertheless be stated that he was only an anarchist in matters of Western politics, and not in matters of religion nor the politics of the East.

Notes on Islam

L'Initiation, No. 11, August 1902

THE CURRENT STATE OF AFFAIRS between East and West may at first glance appear as grave and unsettling, yet anyone who believes that the power of Allah encompasses both good and evil, should neither be surprised nor disheartened. All is providential, and wherever man blasphemes, desecrates, and destroys, there the Beneficent, the Merciful, also spreads His blessings. Across the deaths and the ruins, fates are fulfilled according to the obscure law of the eternal equilibrium and the ways of mystery. Thus, far beyond the storms and cataclysms, the vows of the believers constitute a cosmic force.

Presume for an instant, that all copies of the Sublime Scripture were destroyed, and every believer was slain to the very last man: Islam would still live on, for its abode is not of this world. God has no need for us, but we have a need for Him. We strive on with the religious obligations imposed upon us and fulfill them with humble joy. Nevertheless, we prefer that our prayers reach the Throne of the Most High rather than to have success in this world. The religion of sacred formulae, the alchemy of hope and repentance, the theology of God's greatness and the misery of man, the profound devotion, the simplicity and sincerity, the initiation to spiritual delight and drunkenness from the inner sensation of the celestial – all this cannot simply disappear.

I have asked myself why Europeans have come to understand Islam so little and so badly. I have found two reasons for this, the first is due to murky politics, and the second is due to the specific nature of the Western intellect.

After the Crusades there was a period of amicable relations between East and West, presided over by the Templars, who alone amongst the Europeans of this age were able to communicate with the Muslims. Thus, for the second time since the birth of Jesus (may Peace and Divine blessings be upon him!) the Eastern spirit came to penetrate the West as art and poetry. This spark vexed the powers of darkness. The death of the "Luciferian" Templars was decreed. Yet, the flickering torch shone on, sustained by Sicily and Spain, which at that time was a benign land, and so the civilisation of the Renaissance adorned itself with the Arab rhythms of the troubadours. As the rapport with the East lessened, Evil triumphed. The anti-Eastern spirit, which was clerical with the Latins and Lutheran with the Germans, got the upper hand. A horrible period followed which ended with an event that was as extraordinary as it was banal – the French Revolution. Ever since, the political equilibrium rests upon the peculiar triad of the Magus, the East and the People.

Now, the powers of evil seek to disrupt this equilibrium, whilst the spirits of good seek to reaffirm it.

After the death of the Templars, the spirit of Evil, represented by temple-merchants and lovers of wealth, looked for any means by which to part East from West, whose union would be the advent of the Kingdom of God.

The rapid development of communications brought about a particular strategy. The East was inundated with missionaries, resulting in a widespread hatred of Europe, which in its turn was filled with absurd falsehoods regarding Muslim society, and Islam in general. This is why the West, being blind, desires knowledge, and the East, which has the knowledge but lacks the will, prefers conflict to mutual understanding and alliance.

Latin thought is directed by a priesthood that has relapsed into paganism and does not wish to understand the East. Germanic thought cannot do so, being too obtuse.

The German thinker, like certain patients, absorbs a great deal but digests nothing. Aryan *par excellence*, he thinks only with an inferior part of his being, which is not amongst the superior human faculties. Protestant and vivisectionist, unless he converts to some form of Semitism, he will always be a man of the winter sun with eyes of chilling frost.

It is by the anti-mystical priest and his two reckless auxiliaries – the missionary and the Levantine – that Germanic materialism impedes the union of East and West.

On the other hand, the East is not without fault. It has neglected the [Greater] Holy Effort [for the soul] (*"al Jihad [al Akbar]"*) and has done nothing to spread [the teachings of] Islam amongst the Europeans, who in turn have been allowed to penetrate deep into the

East for lucrative reasons.[1] But this is only a semblance. In reality, they are unconsciously drawn by an invisible force towards a Semitic conversion.

In spite of my profound ignorance and lack of authority, I shall for the readers of *L'Initiation* seek to devote a few words to the general principles of the Muslims. Perhaps I shall be stating the obvious. I have nothing new to announce. I merely wish to explain a number of well-known Muslim beliefs.

The most striking feature of Islam is its vital intensity, seen above all in its homogeneity. All Muslims recognise themselves according to a special trait. All Muslim works of art or literature bear an original imprint. Yet, each does so according to his own land – thus the Arabs, Turks, Persians, Indians, Malays, Berbers, Sudanese, etc., all still differ from each other. Each one masterfully synthesises his sky and the plot of earth on which he lives with the Arabic formulae. No one is expatriated by the religion of the Arabs, yet they still stand united. I shall take it even further. I maintain that the Persian became more Persian after his Islam than ever before, and that the Indian came to grasp Indian nature far better than the Hindu. The Muslim art of India, despite its rigorous formulae, reflects the country far more faithfully than Hindu art, thereby manifesting the great power of spirit over matter, an equilibrium of a well-established consciousness, a greater cosmic charity and redemptory force.

Thus, Islam is a discipline that emancipates. At once both regional and universal, it places the homeland within the heart of man, enabling him to feel at home everywhere.

It is the only creed on earth that is stronger than any atavism or heredity. I have seen Hindus and Buddhists transfigured after only a few years of practicing Islam. One could have said they had come to change their race.

This vital energy of Islam stems from the following fact, that it is the very essence of the Semitic idea, expressed in its simplest and most universal guise. Now, Semitism will always remain a force, on any plane whatsoever.

In the past, Catholicism was more Eastern. Its effect on the spirit was analogous to that of Islam. With its pagan elements having prevailed, it now produces nothing but Satanists or atheists.

---

1 Editor's note: Aguéli is referring to "*Jihad*" (the "Holy Effort") in its higher sense, that is as the inner, "Greater" Holy Effort against the soul, not the "Lesser" *Jihad,* which is that of war.

A meeting of extremes: Islam and German paganism, be they modern or ancient, both adore strength.

The German knows only nature, which by the way, he also maltreats. He only adores its different strengths in spite of the manure. Germany is also the country with the highest consumption of pork. The Muslim, who has an immortal soul and who lives on multiple planes of existence, recognises no other strength than God. In moments of misfortune, every Muslim exclaims: "There is no might or power other than from God, the Highest, the most Great", and the most terrifying of events comes to naught, as if blown away by a divine wind. Herein lies the difference between the materialist, and he who is not.

Religion strengthens the Muslim by parting him from all that is not God, and by delivering him by the Power of Powers. Islam is a great isolating force, and the more the isolation is perfected, the stronger it gets. Religious contemplation consists of perceiving the world to be beneath God and because of Him, and that nothing exists before Him, apart from the veils that are lifted at His will. Religious thought is also about finding God to be the deepest source of all things. These two perspectives, where the sequential emanations [of the Divine] are viewed from above and below, are both valid.

Prayer allows for strange analogies to contemplation, although one is active work and the other is receptivity, or a kind of passivity. Prayer centralises the Cosmos into the human form and presents it to the Creator through the four directions. He who prays has God before him and the world behind him.

I wish to conclude this chapter on the vitality of Islam with a few words regarding its anthropomorphism, about which the theologians have expressed some reservations.

Religious statues are absolutely forbidden because they are always the works of men. Now, a mere mortal, even if he were the most learned of all the scholars, has no right to impose his own notion of the Divine upon others with a precision as material as that of a statue. No one in Islam has the right nor the power to depict God to his brother, nor to interpose himself between Him and man. This is why there are neither statues nor priests amongst the Muslims. The absence of religious tutelage is the most precious of all human freedoms. By this, the Muslim world is not only equal to, but even towers above, those nations[2] that along with it make up the tetralogy of liberty upon earth. I repeat: statues and clergy in a mosque would undermine the universality of the formulae, and thus be sacrilegious. These formulae, in spite of their rigidity, are the basis for vivid thinking, since they are applicable everywhere, in all corresponding or parallel orders, and constitute the rapport between them.

Now, vivid and intense thinking is always anthropomorphic, because it fills the entire being of the thinker, as much as molten metal fills the mold. It senses the whole organism that shaped it.

*

Islam is the only exoteric religion, which by Canon recognises demonstration by way of harmony, that is, that beauty is the manifestation of Truth. The eloquence of the Quran attests to its celestial origin. An ornamental symbol is the dust on the worshipper's forehead; when he prostrates in prayer earthly dust turns beautiful when touched by one who humbles himself before the Creator. When the atheist says that a work of art is a corner of nature perceived by a temperament, he merely parodies an Eternal Truth.

*

Muslim society is the total opposite to that of Europe. European laws do not prohibit the monopoly of foodstuffs or basic necessities of life. By way of penalties, there are only some restrictions on usury. The poor only have the rights they can take. That is why a revolt in the West is not a sin. All social activity rests upon the exploitation of the poor. Even charity is a humiliation.

In Arab society, it is the desire for the goods of this world that is a sin. Money, that is "profit", is almost considered impure, even if acquired by lawful means. It can only be purified by giving up a tenth of it to the needy. This tithe is also called "*Zakat*", which means: purification; and is a canonical obligation. Poverty is a merit. When voluntary, it is almost considered an act of saintliness. The words "*Faqir*" and "*Dervish*" both mean: pauper. Similarly, the presence in a country of foreigners, students and pious men is considered a benediction.

---

2 The three others are: Italy, which represents sentimental liberty; France, which represents intellectual liberty; and England, which represents political liberty.

The principles of Arab society are both fraternal and aristocratic. The rich, the learned, and the powerful have obligations towards the poor, the ignorant, and the weak. "Noblesse oblige" is the popular conscience of the Muslim nations.

*

Islam is above all a state of mind that stems from a worship that is at once sincere, hieratic, and ritual. Its dogmatic details make no sense to those who do not practice it. The extent of theological knowledge depends on its profundity, which in turn depends on the purity and intensity of worship.

A work of art is a closed book for those who lack taste or aesthetic education. Similarly, the truths of Islam are wholly inaccessible to anyone who studies them with coldness, without the prerequisite sentimental training. An [esoteric] initiation is also, from the outset, an emotional training. One is almost always guided by a Shaykh in whom the "*mourid*" ["disciple"] places his full confidence. This Shaykh cannot be compared to a prelate, even less to a schoolmaster. Rather, he is like a spiritual father, whom one chooses and may leave whenever one so wishes. To leave one in order to follow another, is not necessarily an insult to the former. Far from it.

(To be continued.)[3]

ABDUL HÂDI

---

3 Editor's note: The article was not continued.

·

"A work of art is a closed book for those
who lack taste or aesthetic education.
Similarly, the truths of Islam are wholly
inaccessible to anyone who studies it
with coldness, without the prerequisite
sentimental training."

"In other times, religion sustained the heart and the mind with faith, but at present, it is no longer thus; religion is always the same, yet man has changed; he has become all too weak to believe with the faith of ancient times."

Il Convito

1904

INTRODUCTION

In the entire history of Islam, this article is – to our knowledge – the first one to deal with the Western concept of Feminism from a Muslim perspective. This, at a time when women's sufferage had not even been achieved in the West. Marie Huot, the close friend of Ivan Aguéli, was a leading feminist in Paris and naturally also Aguéli was sympathetic to the feminist cause – a cause he also ascribed to the 12th Century Sufi Master Muhyeddin ibn Arabi.

> *"Ibn Arabi was a feminist. He had esoteric correspondences with numerous female saints of the period and there are even women who have written commentaries on his works."*

In many ways, Aguéli's view of womanhood was highly archetypal and idealistic – a celestial apparition in the ugliness of the world below. In one of his emotional exchanges with Marie, he describes his perception of the ideal woman as one who makes him forget the world:

> *"I love the woman who puts her arm around my neck. I love the woman who robs me of my mind – the woman as opiate, forgetfulness. You are that woman, that is, you could be, as you have proven to me on rare occasions. But then, why are you so complicated, so garrulous, so anxious? No, it is you who cannot free yourself from your memories. That is why you flee the shadows and the silence."*

This article – which is the only one in this anthology from Il Convito – is a good example of the witty and lucid polemic that often characterised Aguéli's political writings.

FEMINISM

Il Convito/An Nadi, 30 May 1904

THE GREATEST CHEMICAL DISCOVERY of our time is that of radium, only comparable with the x-rays of physics and the wireless telegraph of the Italian Marconi in the field of applied electricity.

Radium was discovered by the French couple Curie and as emphasised by [Monsieur] Curie himself, the credit for the discovery lies as much with Madame Curie as with himself, and without her scientific cooperation, radium would have remained unknown.

As this fact appears indisputable, what then are the conclusions we may draw therefrom?

Even without a reason to draw conclusions, we could always state that through all the phases of evolution which the great spirits of the West have passed, there has always been a decisive female influence, which guides men towards the summits of intelligence. We believe that in each spiritual sphere, the collaboration between the opposing poles of the soul – that of sentiment and reason – is essential, and which may achieve great feats by bringing them into unity and balance.

In other times, religion sustained the heart and the mind with faith, but at present, it is no longer thus; religion is always the same, yet man has changed; he has become all too weak to believe with the faith of ancient times. He sought to understand Divine Truth by sensory means, and by the logic of the world, not by the logic of Heaven; thus, faith declined as much as God's righteousness fell into oblivion. Now, God's righteousness can no longer be fathomed by reason, but by sentiment and intuition.

When religion is poorly understood, it leads man more to evil than to good; which is why men become "*Kitâbi*" ["Literalists"], but not apostates.

In Europe, religious influence is almost non-existent; fortunately, this is partly offset by the mental influence of the woman, who inspires men to higher thoughts, to noble and pure sentiments, and to honest and generous deeds. Most men who come to abandon evil for the sake of good, have the influence of a woman to thank for their repentance, since the woman of a man who behaves badly, is herself at risk of being despised and rejected.

I have been told that the same also occurs in the Muslim East; yes, most certainly, but with far greater disproportion.

So, what can be done?

Firstly, one should not draw the conclusion that the Muslim woman is inferior to the European woman; in general, she too, much like the man, suffers the consequences of the intellectual, moral and religious confusion that holds sway over most of the East; now we need her [active] participation in its regeneration; the female influence is thus indispensable for the shaping of human characters, since without the creation of eminent personalities, a future is impossible.

The rebirth of the woman must therefore be simultaneous with that of the man, although in a slightly different manner; the woman is like nature, always providing the right answer to anyone who knows how to ask her – so let us not despair. She must be made aware of her mission, her strengths, her rights and her duties; she is more in need of [proper] upbringing than education – and also that such an upbringing should be highly selective. An upbringing that is both religious and sentimental is a vital necessity to her, that is, one that matches her aptitude; she must know God, her Prophet, and herself; then she must also know that she has been made to reign over the spirits [of men], and that her mere envisioning suffices to cast out the demons [of darkness]. Above all, it is necessary to know the [sacred] science of the heart, then the art of exercising a certain dominance over her husband with a beauty that is more spiritual than material. A woman of heart and spirit is always beautiful, and whatever her age may be, she will always know how to retain her husband's affections. True feminine intelligence is like a [magic] spell, that subjugates [all,] even the passage of time; and a knowledge of literature, art, psychology, and even history, is to a certain extent exceedingly useful, not to say indispensable.

I have stated that a woman's upbringing is more important than her education, yet knowledge should not be disdained, but its moral value should not be exaggerated.

A woman may be utterly superior – the very reflection of the Holy Virgin – and still make spelling errors and not have the slightest knowledge of physics, chemistry, or philosophy. But I would still advise a learned man's wife not to be all too ignorant of the true purpose of her husband's research.

We are most certainly feminists, and we shall often return to this question; I also know that all conscious Muslims share our opinion.

We shall remain silent on the question of women's liberation, since we consider it an absurdity, both in form and essence. Firstly, the woman has never been a slave in Islam, as her freedom is enshrined in the Sharia. If we take the word "freedom" for what it means in Europe, I repeat that it is absurd to grant such a freedom to women, for such a freedom is not granted, and it would be an extremely dangerous gift – like a weapon in the hands of a child. I see, however, no harm if – by way of exception – a woman who is fully worthy of enjoying such freedoms, by her merits and intelligence, acquires it – for she will most certainly put it to good use. Besides, it would be as futile as it would be harmful to in any way seek to prevent her – as an intelligent woman always does as she pleases, whatever the opinions of laws or men – thus it has always been, and never shall it be otherwise.

We do not believe that a governmental proclamation of women's emancipation will have any bearing whatsoever; yet another good speech, yet another *toast,* yet another decorated imbecile; and all such "progress"; and on that day, those who truly know the East shall be well amused. Yet, given the great difficulty of keeping watch over a woman, it would be infinitely more agreeable if she not only kept watch over herself, but also over her husband – in case he wishes to veer away from the path of God; but whilst waiting for such an ideal state of affairs – we shall avoid such folly.

ABDUL HÂDI

"I read the Master's books
    before knowing Arabic.
I saw his very self
    before knowing his name."

La Gnose

1911

INTRODUCTION

In Hermeticism, the planet Mercury is represented by the metal Quicksilver. Mercury is the only planet that is not included in the alchemical division between that of the "Lesser work" (Saturn, Jupiter, Moon) and the "Greater work" (Mars, Venus, Sol). Quicksilver is furthermore the only metal that is liquid at room temperature and represents the "Philosopher's stone" which transmutes the "materia prima" ("prime matter") into Gold – the Primordial metal. Thus, by dedicating his article "to Mercury", Aguéli is pointing to the "Great Work" of Alchemy that brings about a spiritual transmutation into a Golden or Primordial state. The large chapter called "Pure Art" alludes to the main topic of the article, which is the alchemically purified "materia prima" of art.

Aguéli explains the alchemical process of the soul by an analogy to the hero of Tolstoy's "War and Peace" – Prince Andrei Bolkonsky – who when wounded on the battlefield lifts his eyes towards the luminous sky and achieves "a kind of 'materia prima' from which one may sculpt an esoteric mentality". Aguéli then describes the constitution of "Pure Art" and how to utilise this "materia prima" to transmute the soul of the spectator into a Primordial state. One may say that Aguéli attempts to explain how an artist may become an "alchemist of light" and make his art serve a higher, spiritual end. As Aguéli states in the article, "Art is the equilibrium of nature and tradition, not only in alchemy, but also in aesthetics".

Aguéli also makes the Hermetic remark that a union of contrasts is "under the sign of Mercury", whilst the repelling of contrasts is not. As explained above, the planet Mercury – unlike the other planets – does not represent a stage in "the Great Work", but instead a "key" or "prime agent" ("primus agens") which is a direct manifestation of the "materia prima". Therefore, the symbolic depiction of Mercury is often "androgyne", that is, a mixture of contrasts – male and female, solar and lunar – which indicates its primordial nature. Through the Fall, a duality of male and female was created which must be overcome "under the sign of Mercury" in order to achieve a union with God.

Such is the alchemical process which is the underlying theme of "Pages dedicated to Mercury".

PAGES DEDICATED
TO MERCURY

SAHAIF ATARIDIYYAH
La Gnose, No.1-2, January-February 1911

AMONGST THE DIFFERENT ESOTERIC DOCTRINES, there are none that – to my knowledge – contain as many analogies to the Islamic doctrine as that of Chinese Taoism, as explained by Matgioi in numerous works. It is somewhat surprising, since Islam, not solely as an exoterism but also as an esoterism is – I would not say the "combination" – but rather the "equilibrium" between Judaism and Christianity. The Kabbalah may indeed come to serve as a bond between Talmudists and Christians, this is undeniable. Yet, as for the Muslim Kabbalah, it is not quite the same as the "*Sepher ha-Zohar*" or "*Sepher Ietsirah*", in spite of their many similarities.

Islam, in its very symbolism, may indeed have come to incorporate many of the characters and geographical attributes of the two Testaments (even to the extent of having identical meanings), yet its spirit is markedly different. It parts from the other so-called "Semitic traditions" only to align itself with Taoism, or the "Primordial Tradition". Islam has always, even exoterically, rejected the claim of being a new religion, instead it claims the title of "*Din al-Fitrah*", that is, the Primitive religion of the very beginning of humanity.

There is a rather curious tradition of the Prophet Muhammad, which states: "Seek ye Knowledge, even unto China!". We may here interpret the reference to "China" as a mere figure of speech, designating a very distant and unknown land, so as to say that no effort should be spared in the quest for Knowledge. Yet it may well be that the Prophet was also alluding to Taoism, or the *Yi-king*, as the difference between Islam and the Chinese tradition is none other than that of Universal Religion and Sacred Science. In order to bring to light all the points of comparison between Islam and Taoism, one would first have to comment upon each and every line and page of the above mentioned Taoist works of Matgioi and then also upon Philastre's translation of the *Yi-king*. It would nevertheless be well worth the effort, due to the surprising results that such a study may entail. Yet, here I shall merely point out some of the shared fundamental principles, such as: fatalism, transcendent pantheism – which I shall refer to as the "Supreme Identity", the concept of the Universal man, the cerebral attribute of visual reasoning, a boundless tolerance, which due to its very nature is in fact not counter-religious but extra-religious. I thus repeat that the long list of principal similarities between these two doctrines may indeed be extended *ad infinitum*.

The doctrine of transcendent fatalism is wholly unrelated to the current state of decadence observed in the Eastern multitudes. The cause of the latter is solely due to the demoralising actions of despotic governments, as well as the ethnic heterogeneity of those nations. Wherever one finds oneself amidst a group of Easterners who are ethnically homogeneous and free, one shall discover that they have as much collective morality and individual worth as do the foremost of the European nations. The sense of abjection is only caused by government intrusions and is consequently only found in large centres of people, be they capital cities or centres of commerce. Fatalism is the notion that Heaven is the prime mover of all things, not so much directly, but indirectly, through people and other means. Our fatalism makes us consider the course of natural or human history as a sacred book, where we play more or less important parts. A great writer, who claims to be a Catholic, but whom the Catholics are inclined to disavow, Monsieur Léon Bloy, has formulated our fatalism well indeed by the following lapidary phrase: "All that comes about is admirable". It was our belief in fatalism that made us discover a monumental [predestined] pattern to certain [worldly] concurrences. In all of Europe, I found but a few Parisians, skeptical boulevardiers, [*"quelques rares Parisiens, boulevardiers sceptiques,"*] who came to comprehend the true meaning of resignation to Heaven's will and transcendent fatalism.[1]

We find, like Matgioi, that sentimentality has no relation to the esoteric evolution of personality, because it is inherently egotistic.

---

1 The most evident Quranic account of the concept of fatality is the command of Allah unto creation to come willingly or unwillingly. It replies: "We come in obedience" [41:11]. As all things obey Allah in one way or another, everything may be considered to be "Muslim", that is, to be left at the whim of His will. The Tao explains this phenomenon by "The Activity of Heaven".

It is above all a kind of blindness and a perilous muddling of intentions. It is difficult to discern between the universal and the particular; between what is performed solely "for God" and what is performed for some petty worldly interest. Yet the indispensable condition for the very first glimmer of "Esoteric Illumination" ("*al-Ishraq*") is precisely to reserve a place for God in the inner being. It matters not whether this place be large or small, rich or poor, yet it is of utmost importance that it be wholly pure and immaculate. It is exceedingly difficult, in the chaos of present-day life, to attain such sincerity and absolute Divine Solitude, even if only for a single minute of sixty seconds.

If it be objected that the spiritual evolution of the Muslim esoterist in fact consists of the gradual transmutation of "Passion" ("*Shawq*") into "Love" ("*Ishq*"), we would indeed reply that it is not the sentimental man whom the Sufis refer to as being "passionate" or "enamoured", for sentimentality, as per the common understanding of the word, may indeed be useful in the evolution of collectives, as it, when subjected to masterly guidance, could result in a sense of modesty, a certain "solidarity of species" (Matgioi) or other well-known forms of egotism; yet, by its very egotism and lack of conscience, it still contains the two greatest obstacles to an individual evolution of personality; that the term "*al-Wijdân*" may be translated as "emotivity"; that the term "*ad-Dhawq*" (="taste") may be translated as "intuitive taste"; and finally, that the European word "sentimentality", in the way it is commonly understood, has no direct equivalent in Sufi terminology, the closest to it being "*at-Tawajjud*", that is, "the imitation of pure and untainted emotion". [2]

The "Supreme Identity" ("*Wahdatul-wujûd*" = The Identity of Existence) is based upon the perfect accord between the outward and the inward. God is Existence, and Existence is always unique and absolute, as a superlative. As long as the human mind is only able to conceive of the singularity of the logical superlative, monotheism shall be the natural and primordial religion ("*Dinul-fitrah*") and thus be a perfect match for the "Primordial Tradition" (Matgioi). I have taken

---

2 The term "sentimentality" has numerous meanings, of which we shall only mention three: the Parisian, the French, and the Pan-Occidental. The Parisian sense of "sentimentality" is a kind of moral convention, and its use is not laudatory. For the other meanings, check dictionaries and etymology. One sometimes confuses sentiment with sensibility, which is not at all the same thing.

Sensibility is the very basis of the esoteric mentality, for it is the starting-point of the evolution of the sixth sense, through which the I and the non-I identify themselves. Initiatic evolution stems directly from this identification. The progress of sensibility is part of the "Lordly mysteries". It is from the confusion of these terms that most heresies are born. The confusion between sentimentality and sensibility allows a small number of impostors to waylay entire mass-movements of the spiritual kind.

great care not to use the words "pantheism" and "mysticism", as these terms are outdated and may cause regrettable ambiguities. The "Supreme Identity" is a form of transcendent or synthetic material-ism.[3] The freethinkers should have been our brothers; yet, lacking the necessary span, they came to stop halfway, and by obeying the obscure instinct of the "religious animal" they have, like the others, turned into pontiffs, less the ancient art.

Due to its social modesty, fatalism and intimate nature, the concept of "Universal man" (*"al-Insânul-Kâmil"*) in Muslim esoter-ism is nearer to that of Taoism, than to the millenarian dreams of "Messianism" and the "Reign of God". Muhyeddin Ibn Arabi's theory of the Universal Caliphate and Mahdism has nothing in common with that of the scoundrel of Alexandria and other anthropophagi, be they white or black.[4]

The highly cerebral quality of visual reasoning assures that, in spite of the identity of tradition, esoterism and exoterism exist on two entirely different planes. Since they cannot connect with each other, any possible conflict is impossible, except for when there is a profanation of mysteries, in which case it is always the exoteric schol-ars who are in the right. Those who perished in combat are indeed martyrs, whether it be against the savages (that is, the exclusivists), or for the rights of man and the citizen, that is, against the tyrants. Though we cannot regard as martyrs, those esoterists who crashed into the street after they deliberately leapt out from the top of their ivory towers. Yet, we should in no manner seek to judge them, be it for good or for bad, for it is only Allah who knows the matters of the afterlife and what lies hidden in the depths of the human soul.

I am here alluding to the renowned martyr Ibn Hallaj, who was put to death as a heretic in Baghdad.[5] According to the theolo-gians, one may consider his verdict to be both just and unjust. The truth is that he was sentenced justly, though not as a heretic, but as a blasphemer and a madman. Amongst the judges were his own initiates, and many of those who agree with his sentence may still come to venerate his memory. He spoke a foreign tongue that was

---

3 Editor's note: In this sentence, Aguéli is most probably referring to the "Supreme Identity" being a "materialisation" of transcendence.

4 Editor's note: There is some uncertainty as to whom Aguéli refers to by this somewhat peculiar sentence. He may be referring to local insurrectionists claiming to be Mahdis. The reference to "anthropophagi" or "cannibals" is most probably metaphorical for those who cause much death and destruction.

5 In the year 309 of the Hegira (921 of the Christian calendar), a Tuesday morning of the month of *Dul-qadah,* near the Gate of *at-Thâk.*

incomprehensible to the common masses, who got confused and had him put to death. Social misadventures by themselves validate nothing, no matter how tragic they may be.

The weightiest tax in Islam is not the tithe, but democracy and the respect for certain rights of ignorance. We know not what to admire most in the style of Muhyeddin – the boldness or the tact. Yet, illuminated since his youth, the Great Master had a feel for the delicacy of his mission, and he did not accept the office of secretary to the princes of Western Islam, except as a training in the handling of sensibilities. But he is still the most Muslim of all the Muslims, and it is even beyond doubt that it was precisely the meditation upon the Muhammadan spirit and the Quran that awoke in him the esoteric mentality from which the sacred sciences sprang forth. It is nevertheless an error to claim that he was orthodox by way of being a Master of esoterism, for it was only in his function as a scholar and a jurist that he was orthodox. It is equally false to claim that exoteric perfection inevitably leads to illumination, for one may indeed practice the exterior form of a religion for an entire century without catching so much as a glimpse of esoterism, whilst Umar ibn Farid came to rise to the highest summits of spirituality by way of intense love. By this, it must be concluded that the correlation between the outward Path and the inward Path is in fact rather minimal.[6]

We do indeed emphasise that they cannot be compared. The most perfect of all esoterists, the Malamâtiyyah, consider dogmatic discussions to be a waste of time, only worthy of the most quietist simpletons, and instead they seek their illumination by way of pragmatism. It is, moreover, an almost general rule that as soon as one has crossed the threshold of the Sanctuary, one no longer thinks with words and formulae of everyday language. Intelligences that are primarily auditory can only advance with great difficulty upon the inward and superior Path, and all of those who are not visual by birth are compelled to learn reasoning by way of geometric figures or luminous points. It is therefore absurd to speak of the orthodoxy or heterodoxy of the Great Masters of Arabo-Islamic metaphysics, as any confrontation between their opinions and those of the scholars of the Exterior Path is quite impossible.[7]

---

6 I translate "*Sharia*" as the "Exterior Path", "*Tariqah*" as the "Interior Path", and "*Haqiqah*" as the "Superior Path". The last is one is rather an evolutionary goal than a mode of progress, yet I yield for the sake of analogy.

7 Esoterism is either perceived or not perceived. When it is not perceived, not even the most eloquent discourse or the most subtle dialectic may reveal it. When it is perceived, words are superfluous. In either case, discussion is futile.

What then is the ultimate reason for these extraordinary similarities that we have just observed between Islamic esoterism and Chinese Taoism? I rule out a priori any historical affiliation as no authentic document exists to prove it. I am rather of the opinion that the two schools resemble each other because they have in fact reached the same depth of human consciousness. They have seen the same thing, and it is crucial to have similar faculties in order to have similar visions. I do not deny the unity of the "Primordial Tradition", nor the spiritual heredity of the initiates, as I merely wish to point out that certain parts of the chain may indeed find themselves upon an extra-temporal plane and subsequently be outside the purview of historical investigation.

THE TWO INITIATIC CHAINS

One is historical, the other spontaneous. The first is conveyed in established and recognised Sanctuaries, under the direction of a living, authorised Shaykh (Guru) who holds the keys of mystery. Such is the *"Talimur rijal"*, the instruction of men. The other is *"Talimur-rabbâni"*, or Divine or Lordly instruction, which I allow myself to refer to as the "Marian initiation", because it was the one received by the Holy Virgin, mother of Jesus, son of Mary. There is always a Master, though he may be absent, unknown or even deceased many centuries before. In this initiation, you draw in the present from the same spiritual substance that others drew from in antiquity. This is rather frequent in Europe – at least in its inferior degrees, but it is almost unknown in the East. About eight centuries ago, Marian initiations were as common as the other in the Muslim East, as it is mostly pragmatic. The many fragments of truth that are found in the works of many a poet or hero of the West are the remnants of more or less incomplete Marian initiations.

WE AND OUR TIMES

Abu'l-Hasan al-Shadhili warns us of those who call us unto mischief, for one embarks upon the "inward Path" in order to attain peace, not agitation. Muhyeddin Ibn Arabi speaks of the exclusivists, that is to say the fanatics and those who are astray, those who exhort people to be like them, to act like them in every matter, and who disrespect the legitimacy of personal freedom. All things come from God, the disbelief of the infidel as well as the faith of the believer.

Any display of zeal outside the public domain is an inconsiderate act, committed by persons who have an obtuse understanding of the power of God. It is indeed an act of impiety to without a legitimate motive interfere – outwardly, at best – in the spiritual evolution of any man. The delirium of pontification is indeed one of those cardinal antediluvian sins, which makes the bane of the Adamic fall look like a blessing, for it is due to them that the sins of cosmic mortality may appear to be of limited consequence. Instead of cataclysmic chastisements, we suffer the ugliness of middle-class conformity. I therefore do not disregard the fact that it is a serious matter to invite meditative men to look upon the world. Yet, I do not want to trouble anyone, nor to propagate my own personal opinions. But I consider the world to be as much a book of God, as any other. Its signs are strewn all about, and indeed we are such signs as well. All of His books stand and explain themselves, one by way of another, and that which is obscure in one passage may find its explanation in another. Further still, the difference between the exterior world and the interior world is illusory. That which one calls "matter" is not opaque other than at the inferior degrees of Existence. The more one evolves, the more it becomes diaphanous. Yet, even if it be opaque, it is still significant. What would a book be without any paper or letters? Moreover, in almost all languages, there are words of truly noble origins that describe the world and even matter. Yet, nothing better reflects the "Primordial Tradition" than etymology. In fact, nine-tenths of the quietists are quite simply escapists. As the world is greater than their own souls, they seek to shrink it in order to make themselves appear as great. Muhyeddin is indeed harsh on them when he ticks off those who only seek a good time in a small artificial world.

Life is an obligation, we all agree on that. The decadence of the Islamic East coincides with the disappearance of the Malamâtiyyah (the pragmatic Path), and the apparition of quietist paths, whose names I shall refrain from mentioning. And so, there are many good reasons to react against quietism, for its very inaction is indeed the worst of all destructive agitations.

POLARISATION

This world is that of contrasts, "*alam al-asdad*", it follows that the study of phenomena, whether it be of objects or facts, primarily includes the discernment of complementary contrasts, by which they survive. Thought is like an electric charge, bifurcating the subject into two elemental categories, a positive and a negative; then, by way of intelligence these elements are recomposed into an entirely new product, which is of a purely cerebral nature. The soul then takes the crude form and renders it into a crystalline, eternal and hieratic form.

This is the formula:

Idea : Hierarchy
$- \times +$: Antitheses
Subject : Nature

Imagine for an instant, by way of this formula, the problem of societal renaissance and decadence. We see that the most general antithesis of the present is: the past × the future. The primary figure is therefore: Each of the coupled terms can develop indefinitely, parallel to the other. The Present, past × future. Immobile time, stability, the absolute calm of an integral society, the totality of material time. Whoso says "past" says tradition, habits, collectivity. In aesthetic terms, one says: class and style. In politics, one says: conservatism. The "future" signifies: emotion, initiative and individuality. In art: romanticism. In politics: liberalism, at least in principle. Individualism is always futurist, as secret aspirations, rigorously personal, always tend towards the future. If you write your x on the line of tradition, for example, you shall find that the ideal tradition is that which develops individuality by all the means of ancient wisdom, that is to say, by the intellectual heritage of all of humanity. With such a tradition, there shall never be any decadence.

Amongst the Muslim Arabs, the Guru is called "*Morabbul-Mouridin*", which means the educator of the aspirants, or more generally, "*Shaykh*" (= Elder) . The true Shaykh is not he who molds the aspirant according to his own personal image, yet he who, on the contrary, develops the "*mourid*" ("aspirant") according to God's will, that is to say, that which takes you back to yourself and expands your true self. You believe yourself treading in the footsteps of the Shaykh, whilst in fact, you are treading upon your very own path, that is to say the very personal route that has been accorded to you by Divine fate.

PURE ART

The title of this series of articles is, by itself, an explanation of the vast array of subjects we have treated therein. We do not wish to specialise in contemporary aesthetics, but solely to define the question, to show the importance of pure art in esoteric studies, to outline the principles of this art, and to illustrate our theory by a few brief reviews as examples. Plastic arts are, so to say, the graphology of the human soul, as a spontaneous, albeit abstract, revelation of a desire that is highly personal and superior. Their study makes an excellent training in visuality, as well as in solar logic, the knowledge of which is almost indispensable in the pursuit of the metaphysics of forms. In most cases, it lies somewhere between theory and practice. Those who have read Tolstoy – whom I am in no manner presenting as an initiate of any kind – may perhaps recall one particular hero of his novel "War and Peace", who, having been struck by a bullet, gazed at the blue sky astonished, as if he had seen it for the very first time. Such a sensation of a luminous void consists of consoling and rich thoughts that simply cannot be translated into ordinary language; it is a kind of [alchemical] *materia prima* from which one may sculpt an esoteric mentality.

I must nevertheless, and much to my regret, confess that I know nothing of Greek civilisation, yet I suppose that the philosophies of Hellenic Antiquity only used the word "music" in a far wider sense than to simply describe harmonious sounds, and that they by doing so wished to, through emotive arithmetic, evoke a new realm, much by way of what today is called aesthesia. One may indeed state that art is the passion that makes mathematics: the spirit plays with matter. Yet, one should nevertheless recall that in this case, it is in fact the passion that here represents the spirit, and it is mathematics which relates to matter, whose perfect science it indeed also is. Furthermore, matter is by itself science, and science is also matter. Yet, matter, as the "Great Innocent", is – no matter what is said by the clergy – absolutely sacred. It is above all by the grace of the Holy Virgin and the Immaculate Conception, a fundamental and indispensable dogma, without which esoterism would merely be a pacifist reverie, or some deviated alcoholism.

More specifically, art allows us to behold "immobile time" or "the permanent Actuality of the extratemporal and perpetual self", which, in turn, leads to the intelligence of the fourth dimension, whose esoteric importance is all too evident for us to mention.

It is rather common to write about modern music in esoteric publications. I am therefore only following suit, yet in a manner that is far more liberated. I can speak of nothing other than pure art, which is the only one that is of interest to us. That is why I make a distinction between cerebral and sentimental art. The latter, which is more common, imprints its aesthetic effect primarily upon the memory of the spectator, through the association of ideas, a more or less confused muddle of memories; whilst the former makes a direct imprint, without any kind of intermediary, by way of a material sensation, albeit inner, of the pulsating beat of life. Hereby, we note that its superiority over the other lies precisely in the great interval between the two extremes of its artistic vista, namely the abstract and the concrete – as well as quality over quantity – along with the concentration of intermediaries that exists between these two extremes. It is of little use to try to make the profane comprehend the vast primordial grandeur that lies in a work of realism, whose material precision increases as a direct consequence of the abstraction the author makes of his own person in his work, and of the level of effacement his self has achieved in universal life.[8] The intelligence that resides in transcendent simplicity is a line of demarcation between the vulgar and the elite.

Whoso says pulsation says rhythm, that is to say, an action of numbers.[9] Pure art only wields its hallucinatory prowess over the spirit by taking from matter no more than its subtleties and governance, leaving the rest aside. As a matter of fact, matter is ultimately limited by time and space, which is immediately regulated by arithmetic. An English aesthete, whose name I cannot find, once said: "Within art, all things are series, contrasts and repetitions." This is, after all, the very science of aesthetics. When we then, by the principles of the purity of art, for example refuse to see in a painting any more than colours upon a canvas, the esoteric mentality coincides – as it always does – with common sense. We wish to claim that a painting must be pictorial, a sculpture sculptural etc. All emotions that emanate from

---

8 When overwhelmed by bitterness, Cézanne said: "I leave for the landscape." Gauguin left for Tahiti primarily to immerse himself in the primitive world of plain emotions. It was, in a way, a bath of innocence which returned him to the origins. The critics of Paris cannot comprehend that his journey was primarily a displacement in time, rather than in space.

9 It is by the "*dhikr*" that dervishes assimilate certain rhythms. "*Dhikr*" is therefore a kind of "*Hatha-Yoga*".

the subject are indeed extra-artistic, and thus harmful, because irrelevant, even if moral. That is to say, all things that may be stated by art by other means than by the sheer eloquence of proportions, that is to say, an arithmetic harmony of an individual and passionate kind, comes from Evil. This is why a still life of Chardin (vegetables, kitchen utensils) has more artistic value than the gigantic historical and religious machines of our "firemen".

Anyone who despises still life is not a painter. He may indeed be a writer, a poet, whatever you like, except a painter, for that which is referred to as "still life" upon a canvas is similar to the pantomime of dramatic arts.

The endeavour of plastic arts is a clarification of one's passionate will or love by the measured axes of three-dimensional Euclidian space, in other words, by drawing. This word, in its widest and most artistic sense, signifies form, which always implies light, and hence also colour, be it expressed or implied. The perfect identity between what is commonly referred to as drawing and colour is the yardstick of the artistic or non-artistic nature of a work, because the antithesis of line × colour finds its immediate solution in light. One merely has to behold the drawings of ancient masters: in spite of the colours being in monochrome or black and white, they still manage to render an impression of colour.

Their paintings, even when blackened or faded by time, still always seem as if they are illuminated by a particular sun that God has created expressly for each one of them.

In summary, pure plastic art is less a creation of objects than the establishment of personal and voluntary proportions in the full sense of Euclidian space. Each dimension of this space shall be designated by its typical axis. We thus have three axes: vertical, horizontal, and optical or visual; I thus designate the antero-posterior direction that proceeds from the eye to the horizon [*"l'œil à l'horizon"*]. I wish to avoid the word "perspective" because it has only a narrow meaning in everyday language: that of linear perspective, to the exclusion of any other. Now, within art, the solar perspective and, above all else, that which corresponds to the mental state of the emotive spectator, to name but two examples, are far more important than those of the engineers.

The mysterious element of art is, in drawing, especially manifested upon this axis. It is its agreement with the drawing on the other two axes (vertical and horizontal) that makes the line and colour identify in an impression of luminosity that bestows life and magic upon a work of art. Its exactitude may never become an object of calculation, no matter how ingenious it may be, whilst the drawing on the other two planes does in fact support calculation and discussion, up to a certain point. The depth of the painting, that is to say its luminous perspectives, be they psychic or otherwise, is only due to spontaneity and inspiration. Either one has it, or one does not. If one does not have it, one cannot have it unless by some unexpected coup de grâce, whilst anyone may well be taught to draw in the other two directions. Such a drawing may indeed have some extra-pictorial interest. It can be literary, dramatic, psychological, anything you wish. Yet, from the point of view of pure art, it will never be any more than a platitude.

The drawing technique of some modern masters is mental. The figure is not what is represented by the material lines, but it is another, inferred, but very precise, which is formed by the tendencies of these material lines. This is the drawing made up by indirectly indicated movements. A dynamic parallelogram will aid the comprehension of the idea. A and B are the expressed lines. They are the components of the parallelogram; C is their resultant. It is inferred, and by its direction and intensity it determines the mental figure that was the object of the artistic endeavour. The numbers of components and resultants of an ordinary drawing are incalculable; I am merely formulating the underlying theory.

The fundamental antithesis whose solution is the very problem of the artist, is emotion (individual love, personality, nature) and style (collectivity, exterior order, tradition). The exclusive perfection of style produces a work without flaws, yet also without merits. Without emotion, there is no merit, yet a personal work that lacks style is a confused muddle of merits and flaws that is hardly any better than a work which is of a style that is both impersonal and cold. Paris wields its absolute power over modern art by keeping balance between tradition and nature. It is only in Paris that we behold painters of the so-called school of romanticism appreciate and study the ancient masters in an intelligent manner. Also, the painters who are apparently the most modernist in appearance are at the same time the most fervent supporters of the Louvre. Within art, tradition without initiative produces only deception, whilst the secret ability to match the great masters of more fortunate times, with regard to beauty, lies in the ability to combine initiative with method, constituting a

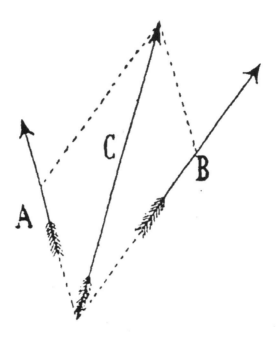

passionate and personal study of nature combined with an intelligence and taste that is formed by the ancient tradition. This is indeed how masterpieces of regal splendour are conceived, since by their personal style they grant us the effect of a collectivity under the benevolent and hieratic order of a single will that is personal and luminous. The purest, the most cerebral of 19th Century painters are Daumier and Cézanne. Amongst our young contemporaries these are Picasso, Le Fauconnier and Léger.

* * *

We have established the profound difference between intellectual and sentimental art. Only the former interests us from an esoteric perspective. It instructs the solar logic and develops the sense of "immobile time" or "the permanent Actuality of the extratemporal and perpetual self", without which the fourth dimension is an impossibility. This art, based on emotional arithmetic, corresponds, to a certain degree, to Western classical music. There are multiple treatises of Islamic esoterism that take the form of explaining the principles of Arabic grammar. The sensibility to sentimental art is indirect. It operates primarily in the memory of the spectator, by the association of ideas, muddling confused memories that may be atavistic or habitual. Intellectual art alone is worthy of being called "pure art", due to its direct sensibility, by its sheer ability to imprint without the intervention of any foreign self or external object, except for the inner sensation of the pulsating beat of life, that is, by rhythm. Now, rhythm is no more than the arithmetic of psycho-physiological activity. This is why the "*dhikr*" of the Dervishes is a vital assimilation of certain rhythms of the initiates. The foremost condition of a sacred or sacerdotal language is therefore to allow the unhindered flow of the rhythm, that is to attain equilibrium between consonants and vowels. The importance of pure art, from the perspective of Gnosis, is the linking of the concrete with the abstract, quantity with quality, space with time, which is nothing but taking matter to its utmost extremity, which is to say arithmetic. This is the art which I call "pure art", for it takes on only the principles of matter, that which is the most profound, most general, and most subtle. We therefore claim, by consequence, that all emotions coming from the subject are extra-artistic, thus harmful, as they are irrelevant. All that which art strives to express in other ways than those of eloquent proportions, that is to say, by an arithmetic harmony of an individual and passionate kind, comes from Evil.

Any endeavour of plastic arts is a clarification of passionate will or love by the measured axes of three-dimensional Euclidian space, in other words, by drawing, by form in the widest sense of the term. Now, who says "form" says "light", and who says "light" says "colours", be they explicit or implied. One may therefore conceive that at a certain degree of spiritual elevation, the antithesis of line × colour fades in luminous perfection. The identity between the line and the colour thus becomes the criterion of the exactitude of the solar or mental perspective. It is the perspective of the emotive spectator, and it is formed by a new disposition upon three planes. Only the dominant one is that which one refers to as subjective, but the rest follow known laws. This article addresses only those who are already familiar with the mental perspective. Those who are not familiar with it would be better off reading something else. Yet anyone who truly wishes to learn of this only needs to study Mohyiddin ibn Arabi. If language is an obstacle, one may study Arabic art. You merely need to look for the reason why the ancient monuments of purely Arabic origins, even the most modest ones, always seem larger than reality. They seem to grow before one's eyes, like the spreading of wings or a fan unfolding. Yet in the absence of Arabic literature or art, one may indeed study the transformation of space that occurs upon the approach of death. One merely has to observe, with artistic attentiveness, the instants of true and conscious mortal danger. Many mariners and soldiers are indeed students of the Kabbalah, and they very often adhere to this particular school.

It is by the resolution of the human antithesis as such, that emotion × style is imposed upon the artist. This antithetical problem has many different angles, that depend upon the existence of various universal forms of opposing contrasts. Some of these are: individual love, personality, nature, innate gifts (on the side of emotion), which stand in opposition to collectivity, exterior order, tradition, acquired skill (on the side of style). In lack of emotion, one produces works of stylistic banality, that perhaps lack faults, but are also wholly lacking in merits. In lack of style, there is a confusion of merits and flaws, which is hardly any better than a work which is of a style that is cold, soulless, and vaguely prostituted. The goal of the scrupulous artist is a personal style, which is the combination of a passionate and personal study of nature in tandem with an intelligence and taste that is formed by the study of past artistry. Art is the equilibrium of nature and tradition, not only in alchemy, but also in aesthetics.

*

*   *

We may state that all pictorial emotions oscillate between Spain and China, as if between two opposing poles. China represents the formal succession of the inner sensation, whilst Spanish art takes us instantly to the novel world of the artist, whose fullness of perspective effaces all preoccupations with the past and the future. Chinese art may be tasted portion by portion. Spanish art, on the contrary, encompasses you with a mental atmosphere of simultaneous rays. Within art, China stands for "time", and Spain stands for "space". I must here also add that without the union of these two opposing elements, there would be no art, that is to say, the progression towards God by the union of complementary contrasts on the plane of formal reality. China and Spain also produce such a union of contrasts, yet not in the same manner: for what is the beginning in one, is the end in the other. The personality of the Chinese artist becomes clearer in the succession of notes, to which tradition makes a great and Divinely inspired backdrop, whilst the Spanish artist manifests his self by the simultaneous accentuation of the three traditional planes of space. From this arises the emotive intensity of his art, from which the forms detach themselves. Within art, Italy is more like China than Spain, whilst France is closer to the latter, and Tintoretto is the most Spanish of the great Italians. Many may perhaps object to my classification of French sensibility, yet here, I may only speak of principles. One merely has to behold the primitives of France in order to notice the vast difference that exists between them and the Flemish, German or Italian masters of old. One may not attribute to them any kinship other than that of Spain.

Nowhere has the union of succession and simultaneity attained such perfection and profundity as that which is found in Arabic art, African art and Malay-Polynesian art. I understand by African art, not only that of Ancient Egypt (sculptural), but also that of the Berbers of the Sudan and that of the Abyssinians. To Malay art, one may also attach certain elements of Khmer art. I wish to refer to all these beauties by a single term: Equatorial art, although Egypt and

Arabia are not, in a proper sense, tropical countries. It should be distinguished from Sinhalese art, that of Javanese antiquity, and also that of the Dravidians, as a certain Nordic element has made them deviate from their primitive tendency. That which distinguishes Equatorial art amongst the others, that which bestows an extraordinary importance upon all of its productions – even the most modest ones – is the notion that it possesses in its utmost sense, which I cannot designate as anything but a "vivacious immobility" ["*vivante immobilité*"], an eternal and infinite character, which exerts upon the spirit a fascination of great calm, whose hallucinatory power is far more profound than the most subtle of narcotics.

The contradictory and abrogative antithesis of this art is (modern) German art. The one, despite its ecstasy, is never sentimental; the other is always thus and cannot be otherwise. The one is always cerebral, despite its intense elation; the other is never thus. The Tropical artist, even a "savage", instinctively knows that aesthetic balance reposes on the unity of the triad of planes, which is the very foundation of the Eurythmic tradition. All the artists of China, Spain, Italy and France agree on this point, whilst the German artist, even if he were a scholar of the highest rank, shall never behold but two planes of space. This is the sole reason for their lack of success in Paris; chauvinism has nothing to do with it, no matter what is claimed. Do we not see how the French public exaggeratingly overreacts to the minor musical qualities of Wagner to the detriment of Berlioz?

The purists, though rather numerous, still form a homogenous group. In spite of this, they are by no means doctrinaires; even less are they pastiche-painters; yet, as they pursue the same goal by the same path, they are, even though distinct from each other, still much separated from the other artists. I believe one may sum up all their theories by stating that they seek the truth in the precision of the light, by the utmost simplicity of means. This dual condensation results in an intense, personal theory, and an art of frankness and perspicacity. Before the work of a purist, one may at first glance tell with whom one is dealing. Only its bias towards extreme clarity should render it, if not wholly sympathetic, at least worthy of respect, for it shall never waste your time.

Within all schools, there is indeed a doctrine (theory) that indicates its goal, and a discipline (practice) by which the goal of the theory is attained. Let us now examine the two in the present context. Can it be true, that pictorial verity may find itself exclusively in the precision of light? I would say that this is indeed the case, and all of French painting affirms that the most important feature of a painting lies precisely in its values, that is to say, the exact and intelligent distribution of light. It is, furthermore, the architecture of space and the equilibrium of the masses in the void. There are in fact formless outlines that may give a striking impression of reality. It is thus that the superlative precision of some principal values may indeed take the place of the lines that give objects their shapes. You may perhaps argue that the determination of the gradation between a white spot and a black spot is not an endeavour that requires the efforts of the superior faculties of man. This is a profound error. Wisdom (*"al Hikmah"*) is nothing but the art of placing all things in their proper positions, of granting them their just values, of rendering them in their truest light. The unconscious (or subconscious) esoterism of purist painters – some of whom in fact realise the admirable type of the transcendent bohemian – have indeed come to understand that this modest craft, this minor detail of nothingness, is in reality the Great Arcane, the very core of orthodoxy, the crown of sacred and primitive Tradition [*"le noyau de l'orthodoxie, la couronne de la Tradition sacrée et primitive"*]. Thus, they come to sacrifice everything for the precision of the tone. This indeed proves that the foremost principle of this school is absolute honesty and common sense. It is deplorable to see them spoken of as pranksters that mock people. Those, who as their sole discipline, have the abstraction of all that which obfuscates their dominant thought, cannot be liars. Perhaps the only reproach of a loyal adversary would be the desire for too much clarity, thus pushing the evidence to the brink of brutal nudity. Yet, to such an attack, one may respond that there is paradisiacal nudity and profane nude and that the Lady of the Well cannot be better clothed than by a ray of the sun. It is beneficial to have intelligent adversaries, who in spite of themselves, still show us the way.

Perhaps you may also claim that we do not properly comprehend the rapport between the self and the perceptive gradation of white and black. I say that the light of the common Sun is not perceived in the same way by all. We have (in a prior issue of this Review) proposed the principle that an artist is he for whom God has seemingly created a special sun. By simple and conscientious labour, his craft specifies the light of this Sun – from his own Sun to himself – and thus the artist attains the highest summits of wisdom and personality. If he then wishes to imagine that his personal sun is in fact the only one in the Universe, I see no harm in it.

This is moreover a matter of intimate conscience; perhaps the innocent mania of this little fanaticism makes part of the hygiene of his craft. There are few things in modern life that offer consolation to an artist; and a small amount of alcoholism – I am here speaking figuratively, of course – is therefore no more than a venial sin.

Simplism is the principle, not only of all art, but of all spiritual activity whatsoever. It is the seal of mastery. Cézanne, with his preference for parallel strokes, from the top right to the bottom left of the canvas, used it as a means of controlling a material element of the work, which distracts the seeking artist from the most transcendent problems of painting. Unable or unwilling to suppress such an indispensable yet oftentimes rebellious material, he instead regularised it by confining it to conventional forms, shaping them into eloquent rhythms. By sheer domination, he effortlessly channeled it into his technical speculations, from which emanated the superb visions that were the glory of his highly intellectual works. The purists of our times have indeed picked up and developed this idea, and thus their drawings, when compared to those of other artists, are what algebra is to ordinary calculation. The reduction of forms to geometric figures bestows upon the work an unusual appearance that shocks the profane. It is nevertheless an ingenious system for an acute determination of not only masses, planes and distances, but also of values and chiaroscuro. By this, one obtains an indissoluble link between line and colour, which produces a rhythmic progression upon the visual axis. It constructs luminous and psychic perspectives in which one finds all things of a hidden nature that may be manifested in a work of art. We have previously stated[10] that the skill to draw upon the visual or optical axis cannot in fact be attained by way of learning, as it is solely the fruit of inspiration. Drawings by geometric abstraction and drawings of the mind are therefore one and the same.[11] The latter are formed by implied resultants whose components alone are visually expressed and are, in painting, that which in literature is expressed as "nothing but nuance" in relation to colour, as in the famous aphorism of Verlaine. It is well understood that this system is not suitable for everyone; one must be well inspired and utterly sure of oneself in order to draw in this way.

The purist discipline renders all sentimentality impossible, yet what is lost by this, is instead amply compensated by intellectual

---

10 See the prior issue of La Gnose, p.37.
11 *Ibid.*

activity. I have beheld works by Picasso where the beam of light has crystallised into a mosaic of well-cut gems and enormous diamonds of extraordinary transparency. Yet I have also beheld, by the very same master, drawings that would be in the proximity of the great Italians. It is by way of purism that we shall eventually discover the secrets of Ancient art – the Greek, the Arab, the Gothic and the Renaissance. Picasso has managed to evolve the entire aesthetics of Ancient Spain by twisting it into the tenderness and immaculateness of Polynesia. Le Fauconnier possesses all the magnificent qualities of the primitive Frenchmen of old, with an added touch of modernity. Léger picked up the aesthetic problem that haunted Ingres, who sought the secret of Raphaël, who in turn, sought the ideal of the Greeks. Now, whilst remaining true to himself, Léger expressed the beauties pursued by Ingres. It goes without saying that the purist of our times has indeed removed all the elements of "guitar" in his "play".

When we state that art is the union of contrasts, we speak especially of the union of mutually complementary contrasts, above all those of "time" and "space", of "succession" and "simultaneity". Mutually abrogative contrasts therefore lie outside the scope of the subject, as they are beyond the influence of Mercury. We may thus summarise by clearly and definitely stating that rhythm is a unifying series of linear and dynamic contrasts; that values, the contrasts between the light and the dark, are none other than rhythms in the depth of the direction of the visual axis. This is why the perfect gradation of values suddenly evokes the other rhythms, those that evolve in the direction of the other axes, the horizontal and the vertical, which constitutes form in the ordinary sense of the word. The contrasting of complementary colours is, for good reason, neglected by the purists, due to the famous theory about them – the theory that has poisoned an entire generation of painters – it is no more than a laboratory theory. Conversely, they [the purists] attentively observe the contrasts between "muted" and "sonorous" colours, contrasts that are of far greater importance that those between, say, "green" and "red", as they at times resemble a conflict between the active and inert, or similarly, between "life" and "death". The purist movement is thus a modern manifestation of the eternal principle of "art for art's sake". One may consider Cézanne as its founder, who, in turn, continued the tradition of Chardin.

ABDUL HÂDI

*"Wisdom ('al Hikmah')
is nothing but the art of
placing all things in their
proper positions, of granting them their just values,
of rendering them in their
truest light."*

INTRODUCTION

In Hermeticism, the Sun or Sol, is represented upon earth by Gold. The Sun stands for the "Greater work" (along with Mars and Venus), through which, according to Aguéli "the world regains its primitive sense of purity and truthfulness by the solution of antitheses through magnificent serenity". "Pages dedicated to the Sun" was published after "Pages dedicated to Mercury" – and not entirely by chance. Whilst Quicksilver or Mercury is a "means" by which to attain the "materia prima", Gold or Sol is the "end" – the goal of the alchemical process. In "Pages dedicated to Mercury", Aguéli described the process by which to attain the "Pure art" ("materia prima") and now he explains how that "materia prima" may be transmuted into Gold or Sol – that is, the ultimate Primordial state.

When Aguéli states "to be, is to shine" he means that by entering into the Sun and dissolving in the Divine Light, the soul may transmute into its Golden Primordiality or "Illuminated Self". Such a state is, according to Aguéli, attained by "Universal man" in a state of "non-time". "The perpetual union of contrasts...", that is, the state of transmuted Gold "... makes one drink from the Fountain of Youth as the world regains its primitive sense of purity and truthfulness by the solution of antitheses in magnificent serenity. The earth then comes to have the brilliance of a dazzling sea".

At the end of the article, Aguéli includes a cryptic passage under the heading of "Documents". Much like his mother's kin Emanuel Swedenborg, also Aguéli claimed to have powers of clairvoyance and in the cryptic lines at the end of this article he describes his visions.

He mentions how he, as a child, in the midst of the Swedish winters had visions of tropical forests. And then, how he as a youth in Paris, used to frequent the "great sombre palace" of the Louvre. Standing before a statue of the Lioness Sekhmet, the idol faded in a vision of the monotheistic desert and the light of the "African sun". It concludes by alluding to his dream-vision of Ibn Arabi in 1893 in Paris. Aguéli's encounter with Ibn Arabi is what in Sufi terminology is commonly referred to as an "uwaysi" initiation. This is when a person is initiated in a vision or dream by a Sufi Shaykh beyond the limits of time or space.

Pages Dedicated to the Sun

Sahaif Shamsiyyah
La Gnose, No.2, February 1911

I

THE ARAB SCHOOL OF MUSLIM ESOTERISM – which is markedly different from the corresponding Persian school – is essentially synthetic. It is, without doubt, the best example of what I would refer to as "lucid mysticism". It is not only scholastic, or rather logical, but also psychological and, above all, natural or primitive. In other words, it considers man and nature as sacred books, like the historical or scriptural revelations that have been expressed in the simple language of the Semites. The passages of the Quran that support this claim are too numerous to be quoted in this discourse. It is less known that the great Masters of Muslim esoterism refer to the terms of "a chapter" ("*Risalah*"), "a copy" ("*Nuskah*") and "a book" ("*Kitab*"), as three different aspects of the initiate.

Geography teaches us that the Arabo-Eritrean countries are hot and dry, and that their inhabitants are distinguished by their lyrical faculties. This is enough documentation for us to be able to explain their religious philosophy.

Lyrical intensity leads to a mental state of "subjectivity", which translates into a somewhat naive enthusiasm that accompanies a good dose of skepticism and finesse.

"You should be naive as doves and subtle as serpents", it is stated somewhere in the Holy Writ of the Christians. These two sentiments, which are incompatible with modern life, settle well with the spirit of Muslims who are erudite and of the old school. Full of vitality, they love. Yet, as far as intellectual tendencies are concerned, they are somewhat ideological. They believe that, fundamentally, man cannot know other than what he states. The doctrine of the

Logos, to them, is less a result of religious piety than the subconscious awareness that primitive men indeed have of the Unfathomable. In the interaction between words and matter, it seems natural to the poets that the mysteries of creation may be analogous to those of speech. Thus, metaphysics follows the movements of the subconscious – especially when awakened for the very first time – and the functioning of thought becomes nearly as interesting as thought itself. Ignorance and the unconscious ultimately symbolise nothingness and night; by which one may then imagine that the world is born along with the day. When our primitive man sees nothing, he says there is nothing. To be, is to be seen, and then to see, for it is the light that grants existence to things. The Sun not only illuminates the world, but also grants to the objects their respective forms. The great Sun over there is almost unknown here; barely visible for a few days in a year favoured with exceptionally good weather. It glows with such an intensity that its very brilliance makes the local colours fade away, so that we see only its own, that is to say, itself and nothing but itself. The landscape transforms so swiftly, that it appears as no more than a mere pretext for a solar demonstration, or, if you so wish, a cosmomorphic theophany. One sees nothing but the reflections of the sky; that the details of the landscape may well be outside their heliophoric function ceases to be of interest.

All things, up to the perspective itself, up to the distances and rapports of things among themselves, depend upon nothing but that radiant star, which, as the absolute master of the horizons, sculpts the mountains in its own guise and imposes its subjecting and architectural will on the masses of immensity.

The power of the Sun enlightens us about the Chinese perspective. It is aestival, in no manner erroneous. The more that is granted by the Sun, the more the sky appears as elevated and astounding, the horizon vast and profound, whilst that which is before one's feet, the foreground, becomes neutral and restricted. The inverse transpires in the wintry or Nordic perspective. There, the foreground expands to the detriment of the others; nearby objects take on great importance; whilst that which is at eye-level, the horizon, contracts and diminishes; the sky subsides.

We have indeed stated that "to be, is to shine". In principle, an illuminated object, when perceived as white, appears greater than its given nature. The primitive painters exaggerated the proportions of all that which had a dominating position in the painting. From the point of view of Muslim esoterism, existence is an attentive distinction, and creation is the act of clarification. The more something is characterised by its attributes, qualifiers or particles – be they explicit or implied – the more it is concrete, real, "existing", as existence, from our point of view, is made up of gradations. An idea is in fact realised only when its latent faculties are brought to light, when all its resources attain value, and when all its forces may play out their game. It grows in all directions, it multiplies indefinitely, yet it still remains "One", that is to say, as itself. The concept of "unity in multiplicity and multiplicity in unity"[1] has the same position in Arabo-Muslim esoterism, as the Cross does with the Christians. Instead of sculpting the figure of a dead man lying across two overlapping bars, we state that "the divine station is that which unites contrasts and antinomies".[2] One attains this station, that is to say, this degree of initiation, by "*al-Fanâ*", that is, by the annihilation of the lower Self. "*al-Fanâ*" is not without analogy to the Hindu "Nirvana", but only as per the meaning given to it by the Bhagavad-Gita, as "*al-Fanâ*" can and must be felt in the course of ordinary life. In this case, it appears as tolerance, impartiality, selflessness, abstraction, self-sacrifice, self-discipline and active fatalism.

We may discern two aspects of Divine unity: (1) neutral and absolute unity; (2) primitive unity, which is the basis of all arithmetic. These two aspects are, so to say, the two graphic sides of the number "one": the incalculable zero, and the incalculable indefinite. From a human perspective, absolute unity is an emotion, to which intelligence cannot grant any direct or suitable form whatsoever. The other, that which runs through the numbers by multiplying them up to the incalculable, contains all the aspects of Divinity, which practical theology refers to as the "*Asrar rabbaniyah*" (the Lordly mysteries). To the Absolute, it is the reverberating surface with innumerable facets which magnifies whatever creature is mirrored in it. This unity is only perceptible by the superlative state of individual initiation. Yet the world is, by its very nature, resistant to the postulates of all the prophets of the race of Shem. It shall never comprehend that extreme discernment may only be realised in extreme universality, and that the paroxysm of the self may indeed be the very height of altruism. Just as the aesthetic works of minor intellects fail to capture the stunning beauty of the simple

---

1 "*Al-wahdatu fil-kutrati wal-kutratu fil-wahdati*".
2 "*Al-maqâmul-ilahi, hoa maqâm ijtimâ-ad-chiddaini*".

proportions that traverse the rough stone-wall of an ancient Saracen fortress, similarly, the bourgeois man is for sheer biological and anatomical reasons unable to comprehend that the utmost conceivable aristocracy is the ideal of the enlightened democrat.

What I place above all else, that which is everything to me, that is my God; God is that which distracts me from all that is not He. They who do not know how to pick themselves up on any given point of existence, they alone are the atheists, as faith, in short, is ultimately none other than the height of transcendent distraction. There is absolutely no religion other than that of intensity, and its dogmas are mathematical.

We must equally discern the two elements of religious life that are formulated by unity and duality. "The One" is the Divine superlative. It is the object of worship for true monotheists. "The Two" is the Divine reciprocity, about which play the Lordly mysteries and the great spectacle of universal glistening. The laws of this catadioptricity are, essentially, obscure; they can hardly be known other than in strictly personal cases.[3]

In our landscapes, objects, however ephemeral, are beautiful, as they carry a piece of the beauty of the day. The more they contribute to the irradiated coruscation of the dazzling ambience, the more beauty they possess. By themselves they are nothing, and they exist only to the extent that they carry the light. When one contemplates them in isolation, they may appear as real, but that is an illusion. Yet this illusion is not diabolical, as some schools claim. It is, on the contrary, sacred to such a degree that religion, under the threat of heresy and the chastisements of the afterlife, obliges us to think of it as such. The Sacred Law of Islam, the "*Sharia*" (= the great Path, the exterior Path) encompasses material life with rites, ceremonies and various considerations and obligations, solely to teach us that things exist, how they exist and the proper measure of respect due to their existence.[4] The canonical laws of Islam are, without doubt, a social order, but above all they are a magnificent treatise on symbolism which assigns each thing to its proper place in the universal hierarchy. The speculative theology of the great Arab initiators seeks to prove that things are in fact theophores, in order

---

3 Editor's note: By "catadioptricity" Aguéli means something relating to the reflection and refraction of light.

4 Initiators of the North exhort us to believe in God, for one does not see Him directly. Those of the South need to exhort us to believe in things. Both explain the invisible according to circumstance.

to make us interested in material life, in a different way than that of ferocious beasts. I allow myself to point out that the mere practice of religion leads to scientific notions in the disciplinary or doctrinal order, whilst the enlightened speculation of the great Masters kindles an inner flame that is the supreme force of all activity.

Let us now return to the landscape. We have determined that the excess of light bestows upon it the aspect of a magical illusion that is wholly unique to it, and that one has the sensation of walking amongst things that are not real. All things are extraordinary. Each day, — what am I saying? — every hour, you gaze upon things as if you had seen them for the very first time. Hence, the gaze never ceases to be immaculate and fresh like the Houris of the celestial gardens,[5] and the soul shall never age. It is the perpetual union of contrasts that makes one drink from the Fountain of Youth as the world regains its primitive sense of purity and truthfulness by the solution of antitheses in magnificent serenity. The earth then comes to have the brilliance of a dazzling sea. The light and diaphanous element, the air, is immobile and grave. The Sun, which is just above one's head, fully enwraps you like the chastisements of an angered God, and shadow exists no more. In its place, there are morsels of night under the light of the moon.

II

I believe I am formulating the ontological principles of Arabo-Muslim esoterism, by stating that the tangible Universe is none other than an immense hallucination that is collective, hereditary and inveterate. One could well say that humankind, through auto-suggestion for generations, is merely playing out a spiritualist seance, and the gravest occurrences of human or natural history, when considered on their own, are nothing but the convulsive jolts of a seance table. Not only are our joys and sorrows no more than false sensations, regulated by long-time ancestral habits, but furthermore it is the sensory conventions of nearly everyone around that has granted matter its traits in the present day. It is not the environment that has created man. It is man who has created the environment by the crystallisation of his extroverted subconsciousness. When, subsequently, the environment comes to influence the individual, it is no more than a means by which the collectivities of past and present times come to possess the individual, thus reducing him to the most ignoble slavery, preventing

---

5 The singular masculine "*Ahwaru*" means someone with very dark eyes.

him from seeing with his own eyes, hearing with his own ears, acting on his own initiative, and, above all, from loving with his own heart. It renders him so unspeakably vile, that he no longer even deserves to be punished for his crimes. When one speaks of the State versus the individual it only makes half-sense. It should be perceived as all of humanity versus a single person, who for his own pleasure breaks the hypnotic chain of universal idiocy.

The common trait of all servile habits is "time". Now, time by itself is sacred, for it is one of the foundations of the world, which in principle is the great purity, which is also indicated by its name. It is the foundation of the successive serialisations, and an exoteric tradition ("*Hadith*") does indeed forbid us to malign the age, for "the age is God".[6] On the other hand, all that is transitory is null and void. "*Ad-dahru*" (the Age) takes on the meaning of all ages, that is, indefinite time, the fatum.[7] Here, it also signifies that which is invariable in the passing of the ages, that which is constant, and thus constantly true. Sacred scriptures are sometimes called "God", primarily as an ellipsis,[8] and then because they tell of events that may indeed be doubted from the viewpoint of ancient history, but which occur all the time in the inner world. In this order of ideas, the materia prima of all that is commonly referred to as the supernatural – which I would call the non-time – is understood as the logical conception of time as an antithesis, the negative value, as the "minus" sign (–) in accounting; as if saying: $\pm(n)$.[9]

One escapes the tyranny of the collective by the

---

6 "*Ad-dahru Allah*".

7 Editor's note: "fatum" standing for "fate" or "destiny".

8 (The Book of) God.

9 Non-time is not a figure of speech, as it refers to a substance outside the limited form that time has bestowed to creation. I say substance, because it is positive on the other side of the limitation [of time], albeit negative on this side. It is, nevertheless, perceptible in the present world. One may even train oneself to sense only that, but I would not recommend such an exercise to anyone. Not only Semitic spiritualism, but also black magic, is based upon non-time. The study of this phenomenon is beyond the scope of this work.

It is by the observation of antitheses, – contrasts or contradictions – that abstract ideas are formed without which no thought is possible. By the exact calculation of negative or imaginary values, one realises this hyperreality which is mistakenly called nothingness. All Semitic philosophy commences in the negative. According to the chronometry of the peoples of this race, the 24-hour solar evolution begins at night, from the setting sun, and continues throughout the day. They do not say "day and night," but "night and day," as it says "night and morning" in Genesis. Similarly, the Muslim Credo commences with a negation: "*Lâ ilaha*" (=there is no god), to be followed by an affirmation: "*Illallah*" (= other than God). The commencement is nihilistic, the end is mystical. But the lucid mysticism of the "Supreme Identity" should not be confused with those schools of past and present times that are commonly referred to as mysticism or neo-mysticism, etc. We replace theology with mathematics.

disintegration of the particularities of time. Past, present and future unite by turning into motionless time.[10] Yet, I neither want, nor am I obliged to occupy myself with these elements of sentimental pedagogy. Whoever wishes to learn about these merely has to open the catechism of any "*Tariqah*" or Islamic congregation.[11]

The highest degrees of the mystical science of time, which constitutes the permutation of time into space and vice versa, are the most suitable for metaphysical research. At first, the question is more abstract, more cerebral, less attached to personal experience. Then, numerous leading scientists, even academics, have touched upon it in admirable treatises on hyperspace. The fourth dimension is seen as a mental state characterised by the ubiquity of man through the union of time and space. The subject is, despite its appearance, logical or rather mathematical, and any serious artist comprehends this problem when he alters his successive impressions into simultaneous notes, since the simultaneity is already an embryo of space. I mention these technical and simple matters solely to sketch all the possible settings of our subject.[12]

Hyperspace offers a glimpse of non-time, which in its turn, opens the door to the only reality that truly exists in the tangible Universe. Two great men of different races, eras and religions have given this material reality – which is far beyond the sidereal plane, and for which non-time is something of a vehicle – a formula of such lapidary qualities that it would be sheer vandalism to seek to alter it.

One of these two is the extraordinary Arabo-Hispanic thinker Mohyeddin ibn Arabi,[13] most rightly given the epithet "*as-Sheikul-Akbar*", that is to say the Greatest of all the Masters of Muslim intellectuality. The other is the venerable Celtic writer Villiers de l'Isle-Adam. I believe that, amongst all known authors, only they speak of "the sensation of eternity".[14] By this phrase they

---

10 See La Gnose, the review of esoteric studies, January 1911, pp.33-34.

11 Whilst awaiting the external reorganisation of the ancient order of the Malâmatiyah, one may with advantage consult the books of the Shâdhilites, Qâdirites or the Naqshbandis. The Shâdhilite authors are the most remarkable of them all.

12 See the journal Il Convito, Cairo, July-August 1907, p.96 of the Italian part and p.100 of the Arabic part: "*Si comincia con volgere la successione in simultaneità. Ecio che chiamasi volgarmente cangiar il tempo in spazio e vice versa... Io ho scelto il termine più generale, più astratto e più metafisico. Ma il termine arabo corrente è : la facolta di veder il passato nel presente...*"
In the Arabic page 100, I wrote : "*Tabdîluz-zamâni makânan walaksu*".

13 See, in the journal Il Convito, the series of articles entitled "*Al-Akbariyah*".

14 "*Al-Hissul-Azali*". In some manuscripts, "*Al-Hissu bil-Azal*" can be found. The context gives the two formulas the same meaning. A hero of Villiers says: "the sensation of my eternity" (Morgane).

both indicate an indestructible and exceedingly subtle element which God has placed in the soul of every being, and which is rigorously personal to him, so as never to be duplicated. We call this *"as-Sirr"* (= the occult, the mystery), since it is the unique secret between each creature and his Lord. It is an enigma whose solution lies in the gathering of vital efforts, so as to constitute a cosmic duty of the highest order. No one can know what constitutes the Lordly secret of another, and the slightest offense against the ineffable celestial signature that each being carries within him, is indeed a crime as abominable as the act of murder. The law that recognises this secret, and hence its inaccessible, inviolable and incommunicable nature, guarantees the most precious of the four cardinal freedoms of man, for it is the supreme expression of the highest way of life.[15]

When man has penetrated his Lordly secret, he begins to know the most majestic Divine Name,[16] the possession of which grants access to the sanctuary of destiny. Then he comes to perceive, beyond the collective illusion, a kind of star, a fixed point in the void, somewhat analogous to that of Archimedes. By the force of a certain ecumenical, yet natural, worship, and by the prayers upon the Prophet, this point evolves and takes on a human form, which, by its sheer radiance, brings forth the horizon of a new world in perfect harmony with the place one occupies in eternity.

This is, in a few words, what is referred to as "the cultivation of the Self", and to which we give the title *"al Insanul-kamil"*, that is to say, Universal man.

---

15 This freedom, which I, in lack of a better expression, call the "Lordly liberties", implies the other three: the political, the intellectual, and the sentimental. They are represented in the world by Islam, Celtic England, France, and Italy. It is understood that Islam, in its true abstract and metaphysical sense, should not be confused with the political or ethnic communities of the East, which one is obliged to call "Islamic" in order to have a name for them. The theory of these four freedoms was first formulated in a Parisian journal in August 1900 [sic] [i.e. "Notes on Islam"].
16 *"Al-Ismul-Atham"*.

Documents:

I clutched some moss amongst the snows,
and saw the splendour of tropical forests.

Whelmed by a freezing mist – In a great somber palace –
A goddess of black stone with the head of a lioness –
Made me see the African Sun across scorching sands.

I read the Master's books before knowing Arabic.
I saw his very self before knowing his name.

ABDUL HÂDI

INTRODUCTION

In "L'Universalité en Islam" Aguéli develops the notion of the "synthetic" and "universal" quality of Islam – a theme he first addressed in "Notes on Islam".

Aguéli touches upon various topics regarding Islam's primordial nature, such as the perfection of Primordial man, the human relationship with the animal world, and the universal aspects of Islamic Law.

Out of all his articles, "Universality in Islam" is the one that has left the clearest marks in the writings of all three grandees of the Perennialist School – Réné Guénon, Frithjof Schuon and A.K. Coomaraswamy: René Guénon used it in his "Man and his Becoming"; Schuon quoted it in both "The Transcendent Unity of Religions" and "Sufism – Veil and Quintessence"; and lastly, Coomaraswamy quoted it in "The Life of Gautama Buddha".

This translation was first published in 2011 in "Studies in Comparative Religion" and is republished with the permission of World Wisdom Books.

UNIVERSALITY IN ISLAM

La Gnose, No.4, April 1911

OUR INTENTION HAS BEEN TO DEVELOP, in the form of a solar transfiguration of the exotic landscape, the doctrine of reality in accordance with the "Supreme Identity". In spite of absolute unity, we have seen that from the human point of view, particularly or disjunctively, there are two realities: the collective and the personal. The former is acquired (imposed or adopted), historical, hereditary, temporal, and hence, so to say, Adamic. The latter is original, innate, extra-temporal, and Lordly. It is perhaps more or less obscured or curtailed, but it exists nonetheless. It cannot be renounced, nor can it be destroyed; it is fated, for it is everyone's reason for being, that is to say his destiny, to which all spiritual and cosmic striving is but a returning motion.[1] The first is reality as seen by ordinary men, that is to say by the perceptions of the five senses and their combinations according to mathematical laws and elementary logic. The second reality is the "sensation of eternity".[2] In the concrete world, one corresponds to quantity and the other to quality. The collective reality is often called Universal Will, but I prefer to refer to it as Need, and reserve the term Will to indicate, as far as possible, the personal reality. The Will and the Need could correspond to Science and Being. These terms are not only familiar to European thought since Wronski,[3] but also to a prominent school of Muslim esoter-

---

1 See the *Yi-king*, as interpreted by Philastre (vol. 1, p.138; the 6th Koua; Song § 150): "The word destiny signifies the reason for being of things; to neglect the precise reason for being of things constitutes what one calls 'contravening one's destiny'; also submission to destiny is considered a return. To contravene is not to conform with submission." (The traditional commentary of the *Tsheng*) "Destiny or the celestial mandate, is the true and accurate reason for being of each thing." (The commentary entitled "Primitive sense.")

    I further add that in Chinese, Muslims are called "*Hweï-Hweï*", those who return, obediently, to their destiny. Muslim tradition states that Allah calls to Him all things in order that they may come, willingly or unwillingly [see the Quran 41:11]. Nothing can ignore this call. This is why all things in general are considered to be Muslim. Those beings who go to Him willingly are called Muslims in the true sense of the word. Those who do not go to Him – that is to say those who do not follow their destiny but are forced, despite themselves – are the infidels.

2 See La Gnose, 2nd year, No. 2, p.65.

3 According to Warrain, La Synthèse concrètet, p.169.

ism currently present in India. Science and Being is literally "*al-Ilmu wal-Wujûd*", the two primordial aspects of Divinity. It need hardly be repeated that it is the Will alone that truly exists in a positive sense, whilst the Need has only a relative and illusory existence. On this point, all the different religions and philosophies agree; and this is why aristocratic natures are to be found everywhere. Thus, as the Muslims say, "*at-Tawhîdu wâhidun*", which means literally, according to the commentary: "The doctrine of the Supreme Identity is, in essence, everywhere the same", or even "The theory of the Supreme Identity is always the same". But here I would wish to insist on a distinguishing feature of Islam, on the crucial concept of the Prophet Muhammad. The Will can attain perfection only through the Need: through having, on the one hand, a need of the Celestial, and through striving, on the other hand, to respond to the legitimate need of the collective reality. Thus it is that Need is indispensable to salutary striving, as a means of developing the latent faculties of the Will. The negative inertia of the former is no less indispensable than the positive energy of the latter. The one has as great a need of receiving as the other has a need of bestowing. They are hence interdependent, the one unto the other. In those rare cases where they function as intended, it is difficult to determine which of them is the most important.

On the plane of humanist and romantic psychology, the personal reality corresponds to Don Quixotesque elements, whilst the collective reality corresponds to those of Sancho Panza. The immortal masterpiece of Cervantes must be considered as a confession of the impotence of Christianity (at least of the forms with which we are familiar today). Has this religion ever been both Catholic (that is to say esoteric, Eastern) and Roman (exoteric, Western)? It has never been able to be the one without forsaking the other. What of those Christians who have no allegiance to Rome, are they truly Christian? I do not know. When a religion declares with all seriousness that its rituals and dogmas have neither a sense of mystery nor of the inward, it makes a public profession of superstition and deserves no less than to be sent to a museum of antiquities.

Europe has made several attempts to merge Don Quixote and Sancho Panza into a single personage. They have all failed, since those few who did succeed parted from Christianity by founding free-thinking. I shall mention only two extremes of these failed attempts, the satanic and the grotesque: The Jesuit and Tartarin de

Tarascon. There is but one Westerner who managed to resolve this problem: Saint Rabelais. But since he was an initiate, he most probably knew that throughout the centuries the solution lay with the Malamâtiyyah. In order to illustrate our analysis we can contrast the Malâmati with Tartarin. The former shows his Sancho Panza whilst hiding his Don Quixote in his inner depth, as a kind of thought at the back of his mind which always haunts him but is never pronounced. The hero of Daudet, on the other hand, exposes his Don Quixote in the far-off exploits of Tartarin, whilst his Sancho Panza, who is Tartarin in private, is dissimulated unto all except for his servant.

The personal and collective realities, the Will and Need, the exterior and interior, the unity and plurality, the One and the All, merge into a third reality which Islam alone among religions knows, recognises, and professes. This reality is the Muhammadan or Prophetic reality. Our Prophet was not only a "*nabi*", or a man eloquently inspired, but also a "*rasûl*", or legislating envoy. He touched the (intellectual) aristocracy by "*an-Nubûwah*", or inspired eloquence, and he prevented the total decadence of the common people and the weak by "*ar-Risâlah*", or Divine Law. A fusion of the elite and the common, the Islamic aristo-democracy, can be realised without need of violence or excessive familiarity because of the peculiarly Islamic institution of a conventional type of humanity, which for lack of a better term I shall call the "average man", or "human normality". Some Anglo-Saxon philosophers do indeed speak of the "average man" or the "man of mediocrity," but I am not sufficiently familiar with their theories to hazard an opinion in this regard. Such a man is always fictitious, never real. He serves as a neutral and impersonal insulator which facilitates certain perceived and expected relations by ruling out any irregular interactions between people who wish to maintain a social separation. Being everybody and nobody, lacking any concrete reality, always being the rule and never the exception, he serves as a universal standard of measurement for all social, moral, and religious rights and obligations. This formalism or this just equilibrium of interests (material, spirito-material, or religio-material) encompasses fully all such outward circumstances as may arise in the course of social and religious life, and it becomes thereby the foremost means of promoting Islam. It is thanks to it that the social norms of the Arabo-Semitic tribe – those of ideal justice, unity, co-operation, and solidarity – can spread throughout the universe.

The perfection of certain truly primitive societies has been noted by several sociologists, ethnographers, and poets. But the virtues of the "man of the wild" never pass beyond the narrow confines of the tribe itself. It remains, therefore, a lyrical ideal only. Its antitheses, present-day civilised man, can hardly excel him as regards human wholeness. With the latter we have quantity, which counts for something, this is true, but their quality is far from being laudable. Formalism, the institution of the average man, allows primitive men to attain universality without forsaking those precious characteristics which connect them to primordial and quasi-paradisiac Adamism.

It is precisely this "average man" who is the object of the Sharia, or sacred Law of Islam. It is very simple when there is no great outward difference between the elite and the common. The literal rule then suffices. But with the course of social progress, the complications of life and the shifting of exterior conditions, the direct application of the letter would have contradicted the spirit of the law. As the average man had different varieties, so the texts were given commentaries, and thus the understanding of the legislators progressed with the passage of life, although the difference between text and commentary is only an appearance. This evolution is natural and logical, whatever may be said by the Orientalists of barracks or sacristies.

Certain Shariate prescriptions may appear absurd to Europeans eyes. They have, nonetheless, their own *raison d'être*. A universal religion must take account of all the various moral and intellectual degrees. The simplicity, weaknesses, and particularities of others do, to a certain degree, have a right to consideration. But intellectual culture has its rights and requirements as well. The average man establishes around each person a kind of neutrality, which guarantees all individualities whilst obliging them to work for humanity as a whole. History knows of no other practical form of human integrality. Experience bears irrefutable witness in favor of Islamic universality. Thanks to the Arabic formulae there is a means of perfect understanding amongst all the human races found between the Pacific and the Atlantic. It is hardly possible to find ethnic differences greater than those that exist between, for example, a Sudanese and a Persian, a Turk and an Arab, a Chinese and an Albanian, an Indo-Aryan and a Berber. No other religion or civilisation has ever managed to accomplish such a feat. One can state, therefore, that Islam is the foremost means of spiritual communication that exists. Europe can establish the international only on the material level. It is something, but it is not everything. Furthermore, it is not Christianity which achieves this feat, but Western positivism, not to mention free-thinking.

This is why we consider the prophetic chain as concluded, *sealed*, since he is its apogee, with Muhammad, the Prophet of both Arabs and non-Arabs. The Prophetic Spirit is the doctrine of the "Supreme Identity", the One-and-All in Metaphysics, Universal Man in psychology, and integral Humanity in social organisation. It began with Adam and was completed by Muhammad.

* * *

The word "*Islâm*" is an infinitive of the causative verb "*Aslama*", to give, to deliver, to hand over. There is an implied ellipsis: "*Lillahi*" (to God). "*al-islâmu lillahi*" thus signifies: to "*deliver oneself to God*", that is to say to follow docilely and consciously one's fate. Now, as man is a microcosm, composed of all the elements of the Universe, it follows that his fate is to be universal. He does not follow his fate when his higher faculties are dominated by inertia. Islam, as a religion, is the way of unity and totality. Its fundamental dogma is called "*at-Tawhîd*", that is to say, unity or the act of unification. As a universal religion, it admits of degrees, but each of these degrees is truly Islam in the sense that each and every aspect of Islam reveals the same principles. Its formulae are extremely simple, but the number of its forms incalculable. The more numerous the forms, the more the law is perfect. One is a Muslim when one follows one's destiny, that is to say one's *raison d'être*. As each one carries his destiny within himself, it is evident that all discussions of predetermination or free-will are foolish. Islam, be it exoteric, is beyond this question. This is why the greatest scholars have never wished to express their opinion on the matter. One cannot explain to the ordinary man how God accomplishes all things, how He is everywhere present, and how we all carry Him within ourselves. All this is clear to the man "who knows his soul" ("*man yaraf nafsahu*"), that is to say his "I", himself, and who knows that all is in vain except the "sensation of eternity". The ex cathedra utterance of the mufti must be clear and comprehensible to all, even to an illiterate black man. He has no right to make any pronouncement on any matter other than the commonplaces of practical life, and in fact never does so, since he can avoid questions which do not lie within his competence. It is this clear delimitation, known unto all, between Sufic and Shariate questions which allows Islam to be at once esoteric and exoteric without ever contradicting itself. This is why there is never a serious conflict between science and faith amongst those Muslims who understand their religion.

Now, the formula of "*at-Tawhîd*", or monotheism, is a Shariate commonplace. The scope that you give this formula is your own personal affair, since it depends on your Sufism. All deductions that you possibly can make from this formula will to a greater or lesser extent be good, on condition that they in no manner abolish the literal meaning; since then you would be destroying the unity of Islam, that is to say, its universality, the faculty by which it is adaptable and suitable to all mentalities, circumstances, and epochs. Formalism is indispensable; it is not a superstition, but a universal language. Since universality is the principle and the reason for the existence of Islam, and since, on the other hand, language is the means of communication between beings endowed with reason, it follows that exoteric formulae are as important to the religious organism as are arteries to the animal body. I have allowed myself to express the analogy above in order to show that intelligence (inter+legere; "*al-Aqlu*"), I mean universal intelligence, resides in the heart, the center of the circulation of blood. Sentimentality does not belong there, since its place is in the mucous membranes of the intestines, when, that is, it occupies the place it should in the physiological economy.

Intelligence and discernment are the two principal aspects of human reason. One conceives of unity, the other conceives of plurality. Sound reason possesses these two faculties developed to their utmost limits and thus can conceive of the One-and-All Being; but this Being is not the Absolute, which is beyond any intellectual operation. One has reached the outer confines, not only of science, but also of the *scibile*, [that is, the "knowable",] when one knows that one cannot reach any further. The acknowledgement of the impossibility of knowing is the knowledge of the Infinite ("*al-ajzu an al-idrâki idrâkun*"). This is the only knowledge, it is true, but one would touch upon the divulgence of secrets by affirming that it is neither a paradox nor a manner of speech, but a science that is real, fertile, and, after all, sufficient. All that is only exoteric ends inevitably in skepticism. Now, skepticism is the point of departure for the elect. Beyond the limits of the *scibile*, there is, however, a "scientific progress", but now the knowledge becomes negative, which makes it all the more fertile, since it comes to reveal our "poverty" ("*al-Faqru*"), that is to say our, need of Heaven. Conscious of our need, we will know how to make our petitions. I say petitions and not prayers since we must shun anything which resembles in any way whatsoever a clergy. It is not important to know how to make a petition, since, in this case, Heaven is like nature, which always answers truthfully when one pleads well—but only then. A physical or chemical experiment produces a revelation. However, if done badly, it will lead to error. Heaven always awards something good when one petitions as one must petition. But it awards nothing, or even something bad, when one petitions in a bad manner. This is an effect of the divine mutuality, or the law of universal catadioptrics.[4]

Sentimental moralists, Christians, Buddhists, and others, have glorified humility. Very well, but to be humble means nothing, since we are all naught. They have turned humility into a virtue, a goal, whilst it is nothing but a means, an exercise, a training. It is nothing but a brief stop along the way, one at which one halts in accordance with one's needs on the journey. Vanity is a stupidity. Misplaced humility can be so too.

We have previously seen[5] how the Muslims' credo commences with a negation, which is then followed by an affirmation. That which I deny and that which I affirm both carry the same name, A L H; but, in the first case, it is indeterminate (36); and, in the second, it is determinate (66).[6] I am stating that the vague is non-existent, but that the distinction is real. By considering only the shape of the letters, it represents a transformation of infinitude represented by the straight line (vertical) (A), into the indefinite, represented by the circle (H), crossed through by the angle (L). For the sake of affirming the distinction, the angle (L) is repeated twice.

The greatest part of practical esoterism concerns destiny, the identity of the I and the non-I, and the art of giving, based on faqirism. The requirement is to follow docilely and consciously one's destiny, which is to live, to live one's whole life, which is that of all

---

4 Life is organised according to *lex talionis*, according to a "*hadith*".
5 La Gnose, 2ⁿᵈ year, No. 2, p.64, and No.3 p.111.
6 Editor's note: Aguéli is speaking of Islamic numerology, where "*ilâha*" totals the number 36 and "*Allâh*" totals the number 66.

lives, that is to say, that of all beings.[7]

Life is not at all divisible; what makes it appear as such is its proneness to gradation. The more the life of the "I" identifies with the life of the "non-I", the more intensely one shall live. The transfusion of the I into the non-I is accomplished by a more or less ritual, conscious, or voluntary gift. It will easily be understood that the art of giving is the main arcanum of the Great Work. The secret of this art lies in absolute disinterestedness, in the perfect purity of the act's spirit – that is to say, the intention – and in the complete absence of any hope of any return or repayment, even in the next world. Your act must in no way be perceived as an exchange for profit. Consequently, it is more perfect, more pure, to give to those who appear to be inferior or weak, rather than to those who appear to be equal or stronger. From an esoteric perspective, it is far better to give to a type of person who is distant from one's own type, than to those who are like oneself. This is why an attraction to the Antipodes, a taste for the exotic, a love for animals, or a passion for nature, are all indicators of an esoteric disposition. The famous poet, Abu-Alâ al-Moarrî, whilst considered by some to be a heretic, a materialist, and a free-thinker, occupied in fact a highly elevated rank in the spiritual hierarchy of Muslim esoterism. To stop oneself at the level of humanitarianism is, therefore, a socio-sentimental error. An initial training (or taming) of animic egotism will suffice for one to be considered by others as socially flawless, since all civic virtues are nothing more or less than politics, that is to say, advantageous. It is impossible, in fact, to do good for humanity without having ulterior utilitarian motives. Charity to those who are like oneself is either a duty, an act of precaution, or an act of foresight. It will thus be difficult for it to comprise anything performed "uniquely for God". Sentimentalism gives an egotistic touch to anything done in one's own name, and transforms it into nothing other than a way of attributing grand motives to the simplest of deeds. The *Malâmatiyyah* always give themselves a number of bad reasons for carrying out any good deed they have been called upon to perform.

The good that one does to an animal brings us closer to God, since there egotism is taken less account of, at least in ordinary

---

7 Here I am not addressing the Ibsennian concept of "living one's life". Those who do not dare, who do not restrain their pleasures, are all too unprepared to be addressed with an esoteric concept. Ibsen, Tolstoy, Nietzsche, etc., are very respectable as individuals, I do not dispute that, but they are of no traditional value whatsoever. They are moralists with a local influence and hence they fail to gain our interest, as they are like small provincial prophets.

cases. As the mental displacement becomes greater, the conquest within the universal soul becomes further-reaching. When you are attached to other humans, they attach themselves to you for all kinds of practical reasons. The attachment between an animal and a human is thus of a higher order. Moreover, it is exceedingly instructive, for according to the following formula: x will stand in relation to you, as you stand in relation to your cat; by this example, one can discover the greatest secrets of destiny. It is true that gestures of loving-kindness towards animals are of great use from a sidereal perspective; but, in order to comprehend this usefulness, one's egotism must have been developed toward the transcendent. The man who realises that the Great Powers shall judge him as he judges weaknesses will no longer need a spiritual guide. He is definitely on the right path, on the way to becoming himself the universal Law as an incarnation of destiny itself. He may have need of technical instruction in order to progress faster, but as he knows how to give without barter, he already has his heaven to himself. One would hardly, therefore, be in a position to label as egotistic those who cultivate loving-kindness towards animals in view of an astral goal, for example, by warding off what is called "a bad destiny"; or to reinstate, where possible, the state of primitive Adamism.[8] These are people who know something, and who use their knowledge to attain a terrestrial happiness which is considered by Tradition as licit.

I cannot insist enough on the fact that the art of giving is the act of the Great Arcanum. The purest and most selfless gift is the sensation of nothingness in the practice of realisation. This crystallised perception is a touchstone – the foremost one – to control Existence in the Absolute. This precious tool for investigating the beyond may appear quite simple, rustic, or even coarse, but it is instantaneously spoiled by a single atom's weight of sentimentality. One could again say "Saint Rabelais," but one can never be too wary regarding theories that are Christian (in an ordinary sense) or Buddhist.

The reader who has been willing to follow me up to this point without weariness or irritation can easily see that humanitarian giving is but the right understanding of our material advantages and disadvantages. Everyone understands, of course, that it is useful for us to be in possession of that which is indispensable for us to live in a human way. True charity only commences with animals,

---

8 Islamic tradition states that wild animals did not begin avoiding mankind until after Cain's fratricide. Before this event, they sought man's nearness in order to be comforted and protected by the great peace that emanated from him.

which is then continued by plants, but then it requires the sciences of the initiates. These sciences will lead to Alchemy, which is the charity of man in relation to stones and metals, that is to say, in relation to inorganic nature. The height of this charity is the gift of the Self to primary numbers, for then one sustains the Universe by one's rhythmic breathing. I hereby allow myself to emphasise that Cosmic Charity presents an inverse line of progression when compared to material evolution, as it is commonly called.

Thanks to the perfect harmony that Islam establishes between the esoteric and the exoteric, one can speak of it on different levels, which is to say that it supports proselytism even as regards esoterism, at least to some extent. Proselytism fortifies it, in the sense that it enriches it from a purely intellectual point of view. It is true that numerous branches of Islamic science were only developed after several non-Arab peoples joined Islam. Many Orientalists, having observed this phenomenon, have attributed it to a juxtaposition of the Aryan or Turanian spirit with the Arabo-Semitic mentality.

This is an error.

The seeds of these sciences were to be found already in primitive Islam. Since it admits rationalism and freedom of thought, it was obliged to explain itself to newcomers, to put on a form which would suit their mentality. This development occurred by the collaboration between students and teachers. Questions provoked responses. The outward need of explaining its subconsciousnesses nourished the rational and scholastic sciences of Islam. The Arabs took nothing new from the foreigners. They did nothing but, so to say, transform some of their gold into coins, their only goal being to facilitate the connection between different peoples.

I invite students of Kabbalah to take note of the fact that, from a purely scientific point of view, one instructs oneself by teaching others; the inward will be enriched by the outward work; Heaven gives unto you in the same measure as you distribute amongst the creatures the little you already possess. But this one must know how to do.

Let it be said straightaway that altruism is an empty word; it should be banished from metaphysical discourse, because "another" does not exist. There is no difference between you and the others. You are the others, all other people, and all the other things. All other people and things are you. We do nothing but reflect one another. Life is unique, and individualities are nothing other than the inference of destiny shining through the crystal of creation. The identity of the I and the non-I is the Great Truth, as the realisation of this identity is the Great Work. If, with regard to a theft, you cannot grasp that you are both the thief and the victim; that in a murder, you are both the murderer and the murdered; if you do not know to blush with shame and guilt on account of monstrous crimes, novel ones, inconceivable ones, that you would never in your entire life have dreamed of committing; if you do not feel that you are some-how responsible, if only in a small measure, for the earthquake in Turkestan or the plague in Manchuria, then you are better off not to study esoterism, for you would only be wasting your time.

It is always the criminal collectivity that demonstrates that the isolated act almost does not exist, and that it is difficult to dis-tinguish one man from another. I do not claim that all men are the same, but I am claiming that they are "of the same". Observe, for example, the following chain of actions. Have you noticed that a general suspicion, although unjust, gives rise to the sufficient evi-dence of the guilt of the presumed culprit? This happens all the more quickly when he is innocent to the point of not knowing how the crime was perpetrated. If he is guilty, but intelligent, he can create around his person a negative, willful aura that diverts the collective aura which wants to overflow it. It is easy to see how the moral aura of a collective gradually amasses around certain nerve-centers in a society, which then are condensed and take on a human form, most often that of the author of a crime. But this criminal is only the hand that strikes. The true origin of the act is to be found in the collectiv-ity. It has done nothing, to be sure, but it makes it happen, which in the end is the same. This is why there are no innocents.[9]

When I declare everyone to be guilty, I am not pleading for the criminal's acquittal. Even less am I calling for the chastisement of all. Esoterism has nothing to do with the code of law, which is a natural product, with all the defects of a society's history. Man can-not exercise human justice in its totality. Divine justice will always remain an enigma to him. To seek to emulate this justice is, from our perspective, among the gravest crimes a man could commit. I permit myself to quote a number of examples. Theft and murder are crimes, at least in principle; hence, the thief and the murderer must be punished in accordance with present social conventions, but that is all. You are free to avoid them or to refuse giving them the

---

9 All impersonal and anonymous crimes are, a priori, collective crimes.

hand of your daughter, etc., but if you say that the man is bad, that he deserves hellfire etc., in that case you are worse indeed than he is, for you wish to seat yourself upon God's throne. You seek to pass judgment in a matter of which man has no knowledge.

Another example: you condemn prostitution, and you are not wrong to do so. However, you can condemn the prostitute only when she commits indecent exposure in public. But her crime is only one of reflex. On the plane of current society, the man is the interior, the cause, and the woman is the exterior, the effect. The woman sells her body because the man has sold his soul. You can apprehend the one, but the other, the true culprit, escapes altogether because he is anonymous and legion. One should restrict oneself to judging facts only. But to judge a conscience is impossible.

One final example: the scandalous acquittals of crimes of passion. Some have wanted to see in them a sign of amorality. This is not at all the case. They are only as many declarations of incompetence by the tribunal. The scrupulous judge avoids making decisions in cases whereof God alone can know.

The universal conscience becomes increasingly fatalist. There is an old saying, "nations only have the governments they deserve". A good government cannot rule a nation of rascals; it will be obliged to be corrupt if it wishes to stay in power. Day by day, one understands more of the great truth by the mere logic of events: that man is always judged in accordance with his own laws, that is to say, the laws that he imposes on beings that belong to his vital influence. There are subtle bonds between the torturer and the victim, for they are two aspects of the same event. Everyone realises that it is because of the rich that there are paupers; that it is because of the wise that there are fools; that there are vicious men because the men of virtue leave much to be desired. Several saints of Islam complained of having been given the gift of secondary sight. They have seen too many extraordinary things in the minor occurrences of everyday life. The naive ones are those who seek super-human faculties outside of the given order. When these sorcerer's apprentices do not fall into intellectual or moral deviation, it means God has been merciful to them.

*

*   *

The law of universal poverty (*"al-Faqru"*) is indeed an Islamic principle. Each one of us is a pauper (*"Faqîr"*). We are all paupers (*"Fuqarâ"*), because we all have a need for the Creator or the creation, most often for them both. As one must give in order to receive, it follows that the greatest misfortune lies in not being able to do any good, in having lost the right to exercise charity. When one gives, one must give more modestly than the pauper who receives the alms from one's hand.

It is above all through its conception of the collective reality that Islam stands apart from other religions, civilisations, and philosophies. All enlightened ones know that the collective reality is a fiction. The enlightened Muslims know this just as well, if not better. Therefore, aiming to follow the Prophet, one does not retire into the desert, but one pretends that one takes the world seriously. A *hadith* states that we must work for this life as if we were to live for a thousand years, and for the next world as if we were to die tomorrow. The doctrine of identity and unity is developed further in Islam than anywhere else. Its most precious quality of esotero-exoterism provides above all its concept of the collective reality as an indispensable means by which it can transform the personal reality into the Universal humanity or the Prophetic reality. Christianity and Buddhism reject the collective reality with horror or disdain in order to make the universal Man exist in a minute quietude. Hence, they differ from Islam in a way that is both qualitative and psychological. Islam differs quantitatively from esoteric Brahmanism, as it is more vast. Brahmanism is only a local phenomenon, at least from a practical point of view, whilst Islam is universal. It differs from anti-doctrinal positivism on the point of formalism and metaphysics. It stands in direct opposition to German philosophy, which, through its confusion of feudalism with aristocracy, has totally distorted the idea of government. Everywhere except for Germany, responsibility is a measure of nobility: the more one is noble, the more responsible, and vice-versa. According to the Sharia the crimes of the free or the noble are judged more severely than those of the slaves or the ignorant. Unfortunately, feudalism is everywhere turned into a system that assures impunity; but everywhere it is kept apart from nobility, whilst in Germany feudalism is the sole condition for aristocracy. The strongest has no obligation in regards to the one whose unhappy fate has placed him in an inferior situation.

In contrast, Islam has points of comparison and contact with most forms of beliefs and social structures. It is, however, neither a religious mixture nor a novelty. The Prophet expressly stated that he had invented nothing new relating to dogmas or laws. He merely restored the primitive and ancient faith. This is why there is much resemblance between Taoism and Islam. I am not the one who dares to make such an assertion of similarity, but it has been made by celebrated authors on Islam in China. Taoism differs from Islam only by the fact that it is exclusively esoteric, whilst Islam is esotero-exoteric. This is why the one can promote its doctrines, whilst the other cannot. Islam knows both neophyteness and adeptness, whilst Taoism recognises only the latter of these two forms of expansion.

ABDUL HÂDI

"The perfection of certain truly primitive societies has been noted by several sociologists, ethnographers, and poets. [...] Its antitheses, present-day civilised man, can hardly excel him as regards human wholeness."

INTRODUCTION

This article on the Malâmatiyyah was a translation of a text which Ivan Aguéli wanted to preserve for posterity. Aguéli very much identified with the Malâmatiyyah and wished to reconstitute its doctrines in the West. In fact, he even stated that the conversion of René Guénon to Islam was partly due to his inclination ("maylan") towards the Malâmati path.

In this article Aguéli explains how the Malâmatiyyah were "liberal" and "democratic" – and that their decline coincided with the ruin of the entire Muslim world. According to Aguéli, the traditional Malâmati stood as a counterweight to the religious "fanatic" of modern times, who not only wishes to destroy whatever is left of the traditional world – be it buildings, customs or clothing – but also strives to meddle in the spiritual lives of his fellow men, to direct it and compel it to conformity.

Although the main part of this text is a translation, it is still included in this anthology as it is a rare text on the Malâmatiyyah and a topic which one must be familiar with if one wishes to fully understand the character of Ivan Aguéli.

AL-MALÂMATIYYAH

La Gnose, No.3, March 1911

WITH THE TERM "THE PEOPLE OF BLAME" ("*Ahlul-Malâmah*") there are three highly distinct concepts that may however be identical in exceptional circumstances. First and foremost, the "*Malâmatiyyah*" constitute a group of great initiates, a kind of "*Mahatmas*",[1] who occupy the fifth degree in the spiritual hierarchy of Muslim esoterism. Below follows an excerpt from the "Treatise on the Sufi Categories", by Muhyeddin Ibn Arabi.[2]

The fifth degree is occupied by "those who bow", those who humiliate themselves before the Divine Greatness, who impose upon themselves the strictness of religion, who are liberated from any claim of reward in this world or in the next. These are the Malâmatiyyah. They are the "people of trust in the Divine" and they constitute the highest group. Their numbers are not limited, but they are under the guidance of the "*Qutb*" or "the spiritual Pole".[3] The rules of their order forbid them to show their qualities and hide their faults. Still, they act in the open and are active in all the areas of the "spiritual virility" ("*ar-Rajuliya*").

They have ten stages to which they return and of which they speak. These are: [1] the charity of Knowledge, [2] wisdom, [3] foresight, [4] the art of judging the intimate nature of people and things by way of exterior signs, [5] glorification, [6] inspiration, [7] the "Great Peace" ("*as-Sakinah*"), [8] security and [9] the elevation of the spirit.[4] They attach themselves to the following Divine names:

---

1 I use this word for lack of a better one, although it does have another meaning in Sanskrit, and because it is well-known; yet what I wish to convey has naturally nothing in common with the fictional meaning ascribed to it by the Theosophists. By using it, I merely wish to designate those initiates who have come to fully master their existential aptitude in its entirety.

2 Editor's note: It is rather unclear exactly which part of Ibn Arabi's *Futuhat al-Makkiyah* Ivan Aguéli is quoting. In the original La Gnose article, there is an opening quotation mark but no closing quotation mark. There is therefore an uncertainty as to exactly where the citation ends. In order not to confuse the reader, we have omitted the opening citation mark.

3 The numbers of "*Afrâd*" or "Solitaries" are not limited either, but they are not under the direct guidance of the "Pole of the Age". They constitute the third category in the hierarchy of Muslim esoterism.

4 The copyist of my manuscript has forgotten the name of the tenth "station". Such omissions occur all too frequently to astonish the ardent Arabist.

The Abaser ["*al-Khâfid*"], The Exalter ["*ar-Râfi*"], the Giver of Glory ["*al-Mu'izz*"], the Humiliator ["*al-Mudhill*"], etc.

They speak of the control of actions (by purification of intentions), of the refinement of piety, the restraint of passions, the absence of pretension with God, obedience to the prophetic Tradition, voluntary poverty, indulgence towards others, the discipline of speech, not only by way of silence, but also by the obligation to speak by God's permission, the Shariate light, etc.

They also speak of the various 'inner notices' ("*al-Khawâtir*"), the Lordly, the angelic, the intellectual, the psychic and the diabolical, as well as the various nuances of Lordly notices, that of Allah, and that of the Merciful. They say that the first stems from 'Majesty'; that of the Merciful stems from "Beauty", and the divine notice stems from "Perfection". The first notice is always true, according to their tradition. In the "disciple" ("*al-Mourîd*"), it manifests itself as the precise interpretation of external signs; as "traveller" ("*as-Sâlik*"), as "intuition" ("*Mokâshafah*"); and, with the "initiate" ("*al-Ârif*") as "contemplation" ("*Moshâhadah*"). The notice that stems from "Majesty" ("*al-Jelâl*") erases and annihilates; that which stems from "Beauty" ("*Jamâl*") strengthens and fortifies; the one which stems from "Perfection" ("*Kamâl*") improves and leads unto the straight path. One prepares for "Majesty" by "Steadfastness" ("*as-Sabr*"), "Beauty" by "Gratitude" ("*as-Shukr*"), and "Perfection" by the "Great Peace". According to them, the height of Sufism is the restraint of passions, the absence of pretensions, the attachment to God's names and attributes, as well as their incarnation. They say that Sufism is humility, poverty, the "Great Peace", and contrition. They say that "the face of the Sufi is despondent (literally "black") in this world and in the next", thus indicating that ostentation ceases along with pretensions, and that sincerity of worship is manifested by contrition, for it is said: "I am with those whose hearts are broken because of Me".

The invocations of the Malâmatis are made up by sacred formulas whose literal meaning indicates abstraction and purification, such as: "Praise be unto God the Immense", "Praise be unto the Holy King", etc. When perfected, these names, by their invocation, bring to light that which they lack, for "the order is that of the Wise, the Savant and the Well-informed *par excellence*". What they actually possess of Grace comes from the source of divine favors. No longer do they have their own names or features, for they have been effaced by "true prostration".

Secondly, the word *"Malâmatiyyah"* refers to one of the three fundamental elements of Islamic religiosity. It constitutes the "Superior Path" or the pragmatic, which includes the other two: the "Interior Path" or the quietist, Sufi, and the "Exterior Path" or exoteric, ritual, moral, and social. The Arabic treatise which we are translating today concerns the *Malâmatiyyah* of the second kind.

But there is also a religious order, a *"Tarîqah"*, of the same name. It is rather rare; it is found only in Albania, Syria and India. In the past, it was powerful and widespread; but, as it was democratic and liberal, it was ruined by government persecution. Its name is still revered among Dervishes of all orders. In times of hardship, it is a Malâmati tradition to take shelter amongst the *Naqshabandiyyah* and the *Bektashiyyah*. The ruin of this order coincides with the decline of the entire Muslim world. Books on this order are exceedingly rare, because its Shaykhs do not like to write much. I have found only one manuscript of the only book I know on the subject. My manuscript is in a very poor condition. Poorly scripted in numerous places, it is barely decipherable. Words and entire sentences have vanished by the destructive workings of time – by way of mold, worms and holes. It has so many gaps that one sometimes does not know if it is a "yes" or a "no". I shall therefore require the reader's full attention, and I reserve the right to redact this translation at a later date, if I ever find another, more complete manuscript of this treatise. In the face of these challenges and consequent misunderstandings, I still risk the publication of the pamphlet, for it is a unique document on an entirely new topic.

THE PRINCIPLES OF THE MALÂMATIYYAH
By the Wise Imâm, the learned Initiate, Seyyid Abu Abd ar-Rahmân (grandson to Ismaîl ibn Najib).

In the Name of Allah, the Beneficent, the Merciful; may Allah pray for our Lord Muhammad, for his family, his companions, and the first Muslims, the upholders of his Tradition. Glory unto God, Who has chosen from amongst His servants; Who established his elect as pontiffs of His Kingdom; Who embellished their exteriors by worship, and who illuminated their interiors by His science and His love. He told them how to know one's inferior I. He granted them the power to dominate this I by making them aware of the pitfalls. He helped them reduce the proud and selfish I to naught, and

He taught them to despise it. Those who obey His commands and know His sovereign Grace, those are the true scholars. God distinguishes by His mercy whomever He wants.

You have asked me to tell you of the Malâmatiyyah, their methods for developing the Self,[5] and their spiritual states. Know then, that initiates of this order do not own written books nor collections of tales, for their "Way" consists only in attaining a particular state of mind, in the evolution of character and in spiritual exercises. I shall do my best to explain the means by which they develop this mentality, as well as all the practical or psychological consequences of this education; this, after asking God to assist me in the course of this work, to make me worthy of my task, and to direct me to the path of truth. That suffices me, and it directs everything to a good result. Know then, – and may Allah prepare you in the best of manners! – that the masters of the science of the heart and mind are of three kinds. Those in the first category focus on the Shariate science of decisions being mainly concerned with the public good and the maintenance of religious law. They collect, teach and explain the various precepts of the law, which regulates all ordinary relationships between people by the distribution of rights and goods. They do not care in any way about what concerns only the elite of the Muslims, that is, their ecstatic states, their spiritual degrees and their visions of the hypersensory. They are the scholars of esoterism, the arbiters of disputes and challenges, who watch over the principles of the Sharia and maintain the religious and hieratic atmosphere. Their competence concerns the rules of good conduct to be held *vis-à-vis* the exterior world, in accordance with the Book of God and the Tradition of the Prophet. These are the "Ulama", properly called, that is, the connoisseurs of the Sharia. They are the Princes of religion, as long as they do not make mistakes and indulge in the ambition and desires of this fleeting inferior world and its vanities, which corrupt the souls.[6]

The second category is made up of the elite of the believers, by those whom Allah has distinguished by His knowledge, those whose deeds and desires have been excluded from all that is not the "True Divine", so that they care only for Him, bring their desires

---

5 That is, all the states of being that constitute the Personal Entity.
6 They can only be wrong in ordinary life, just like all other human individuals; yet there can never be a regression in the spiritual hierarchy, to any degree. The doctors of the Sharia are always infallible when they speak "ex cathedra" in the name of law and Tradition, because they then participate in the infallibility of the Doctrine itself (see "La Prière et l'Incantation", 2nd year, No. 1, p.23).

only to Him, do not aspire unto anything that is the object of the aspirations of common man, and have no regard for exterior life; but they concentrate all their desires toward God, care only about the spiritual realm, and find no spiritual respite in the commerce with creatures, who (by the way) are wholly incapable of understanding them. They constitute an elite that has been chosen by God, isolated from the rest of the world, and favored by various wondrous faculties. They are for Him, by Him, and go unto Him in all matters; this, once they have completed the Path of External Works, kept the "Lordly Secret",[7] and fought the Greater Holy War of spiritual combat.[8] In their "Lordly secret," they constantly look to the "True Divine" and contemplate the occult things of the hypersensory realm. Their corporeal life is embellished by the splendours of ritual worship, so that their exterior in no way is contrary to the Sharia. This notwithstanding, their interior is in perpetual contemplation of the hypersensory [realm]. It was about them that the Prophet said, "Whoso takes God as the sole goal of his concern, God (Allah) shall exempt him from any other concern." These are "the people of Knowledge".[9]

The third category are the so-called Malâmatiyyah. They are those whose interiors Allah has embellished with various wonderful qualities, such as "*al-Qurbah*" or "Divine Proximity", "*az-Zulfâ*" or "Celestial Approach", "*al-Uns*" or "Beatitude", and "*al-Ittisâl*" or "Spiritual Union." By their "Lordly Secret", they realised the ideals of the hypersensory realm and can no longer be separated from them. As they realised (the "True Divine") in the superior degrees (of the Microcosm); as they asserted themselves amongst the "people of concentration",[10] of "*al-Qurbah*", "*al-Uns*" and "*al-Wasl*",[11] God is (so to speak) too jealous of them to allow them to reveal themselves to the world as they really are. He thus grants them an exterior that corresponds to the state of "separation from Heaven",[12] an exterior made up of ordinary knowledge, preoccupations with the Sharia – be they ritualistic or hieratic – as well as the obligation to work, practice, and act amongst the multitude of men. However, their interiors remain in constant connection to the "True Divine", both in concentration

---

7 Regarding the "Lordly Secret", see La Gnose, 2nd year, No. 2, p.65.
8 "*Al-Mojâhidât*", derived from "*al-Jihâd*", that is, the [Greater] Holy War. That which is waged against the infidels, that is to say against the external and aggressive enemies of Islam, is called "the Lesser Holy War".
9 "*Ahlul-Marifah*", that is, the Gnostics.
10 "*Ahlul-Jam'i*".
11 Spiritual union.
12 "*Al-iftirâq*".

("*al-Jam'*") and in dispersion ("*al-Farq*"), that is to say, in all the states of existence. This mentality is one of the highest that man may attain, even if nothing appears in the exterior. It resembles the state of the Prophet—may Allah pray for him and greet him! — which was raised to the highest levels of "divine proximity," indicated by the Quranic formula: "Till he was (distant) two bows' length or even nearer".[13] When he returned to the creatures, he only spoke to them of exterior things. Of his intimate entreaty with God, there was no sign upon his person. Such a state is superior to that of Moses, at whose person no one could look after he had spoken to God. The Sufis, that is to say, the sages of the second category, are like the case of Moses, for their lights and their "Lordly secrets" manifest themselves extrinsically. The Malâmatiyyah, on the contrary, never speak of their spiritual experiences, and teach their disciples only of the different ways by which to obey God, and of truly following the Tradition, in all circumstances. They do not allow them to claim the rewards of good works, nor disclose miracles or extraordinary things, nor to relate to them. But they teach them the true manner of action and to persist in sacred efforts. They admit the disciple to training and elevate him according to their hieratic principles. When they perceive flaws in his states or actions, they explain to him his shortcomings, and guide him to correct himself. They never approve of anything and do not dispense flattering words. If the disciple claims to experience superior "states" ("*Ahwâl*"), regarding himself accomplished, they make him see that his "state" ("*Hâl*") is of a minor kind, until they have verified the truth of his intention. Then and only then do they make him see what they are themselves by recommending him to keep secret the superior "states" of ecstasy, to observe external relations, to accomplish what is prescribed and to avoid what is prohibited (according to external law). Thus, the control of the "spiritual stations" ("*Maqâmât*") lies entirely in the will; the validity of the will grants, according to them, the validity of all "spiritual stations"... (gap in the text; the passage is unintelligible) ... The Shaykh of the order, Abu Hafs an-Neyshabûrî, once said: "Malâmati disciples evolve by expending themselves. They care not for themselves. The world has no hold on them, and cannot reach them, for their exterior life is fully exposed, whilst the subtleties of their interior life are profoundly hidden. Sufi disciples, on the other

---

13 See the Quran 53:9. The two arcs are "*al-Ilm*" and "*al-Wujûd*", that is, "Knowledge" and "Being". See F. Warrain, on Wronski, "La Synthèse concrete", p.169.

hand, have claims to be rewarded for their good works in this world and the next, claims that the Malâmites regard as deficiencies. The discrepancy between their pretentions and their merits makes the critics laugh."

Abu Hafs was once asked about the name Malâmiyyah [the "Blameworthy"]. He replied: "The Malâmiyyah are always with God due to their constant self-dominance and unwavering awareness of their Lordly secret. They blame themselves for all they cannot refrain from showing of their "Divine proximity", by way of prayer or otherwise. They dissimulate their merits and expose what makes them blameworthy. Thus, whilst people judge their exteriors, they blame themselves in their interiors, for they know human nature. Yet God favours them by the unveiling of mysteries, by the contemplation of the hypersensory world, by the art of knowing the intimate reality of things by way of external signs ("*al-Ferâsah*"), and by the way of miracles. The world ultimately leaves them in peace with God, cast aside due to their ostentation of the reprehensible or contravention of the respectable. Such is the discipline of the "*Tarîqah*" of the people of blame."[14] Ibrahîm al-Fattâl told Ahmad ibn Ahmad al-Malâmatî that he once questioned Hamdûn al-Qassâr (= the grease cleaner) about the Malâmian Path. Hamdûn replied: "It consists of renouncing all embellishment of oneself by pretension to the perfect "states" in order to stand out in the eyes of men; to forego seeking their approval with respect to character and actions; so that no blame (on the account of God) befalls you regarding the rights of God over you."[15]

Ahmad ibn Mohammad al-Farrâ told me that Abd-Allah ibn Manâzil once said, when asked about the Malâmatiyah: "These are the men who have no human respect or hypocritical dissimulation before the world, and who in no manner claim that God shall recompense them on account of their good works. Their conduct *vis-à-vis* the world, as well as God, is spontaneous – bereft of all intellectual or sentimental artifice. I have heard it stated by my grandfather, Ismaîl ibn Najîb, that: "As long as the 'mental states' and the acts of a man are [driven by] pretension and ulterior motives, he cannot attain any Malâmite degree." One of their Shaykhs was

---

14 These words of Abu-Hafs were collected by Abul-Hassan al-Warrâq, who reported them to Ahmad ibn Aisa, who in turn was the informant of Abu Abdur-Rahmân, the author of this treaty.

15 The meaning of which is that one should only seek approbation of Oneself in order to obtain that of God. The world always wants the opposite of what God wishes that you want.

once asked, "What makes your 'Path' so superior?" He replied, "The debasing of and contempt for the inferior I; the training to do without all things that grant it satisfaction and in which it finds respite; the belief that others are better than oneself; to think well of them and excuse their faults. Thus, one is compelled to depreciate oneself and diminish one's own merits." Abu Hafs has said: "God has made known [to us] how to come close to Him, the "Divine Proximity" and the "most elevated degrees". I ask God to show me the path towards the "True Divine", even if only by the length of a single step. Abu Yazid al-Bistâmî said: "People imagine the path unto God to be more evident than the Sun, more discernable than the Moon. I believe the path is hidden. I beseech Him to open it unto me, even if no wider than a needle's eye."[16] Suchlike were all the great Masters of this Path. The more truthful and exalted their intimacy with God, the more they were humble and modest; this was not only to train the disciples as per the good tradition, but also in order to consolidate their rapport with the "True Divine", so as to never turn towards anyone "other than Him" and thus invalidate their spiritual state. One of them was asked: "What have you attained?" He replied: "Have you not given up your pretentions?" He added: "To claim a reward for one's good works is blasphemy and mockery. Once one enters oneself, one perceives oneself as lacking any merit, for one is far from God. Is it not like the poet said: "The view of water is painful for the thirsty man – once the path to the drinking trough is severed"? I asked Ahmad ibn Mohammad al-Farrâ (="the skinner"): "What is the Malâmatiyyah?" He replied: "The truer their rapport with God, the more humbling their refuge with Him, the more they apply themselves to the fear and veneration of God. At such a degree of mental evolution, the risks of "Istidrâj"[17] are exceedingly high…..................... (incomprehensible text, because of holes) …..................... What I heard from Ibn Nidâr (?) about Shaykh Abu Hafs still relates to this state. Abu Hafs said: "For forty years, I have been waiting for God to look at me with a favourable eye. Yet, my work indicates that I am unworthy of it." The entire method of Abu Hafs and his companions consisted in exhorting the disciples to works, to sacred efforts, in setting an example for them to

16 In the text, it says: the "head of a needle". This expression is rare, whilst the metaphor of the "needle's eye" is more common.
17 "Al-Istidrâj" is a diabolical ruse that lurks in [spiritual] evolution. It is a well-known and frequent phenomenon; all the Shaykhs know of it. The disciple makes rapid progress, and swiftly reaches the superior degrees; all of a sudden he takes a fall, never to rise again. The higher his spiritual state, the more terrible the fall.

act and do good, so that they would not cease devoting themselves to the practices with zeal, disinterest and assiduity. The method of Hamdûn al-Qachâr and his companions consisted in depreciating the works of the disciples, indicating their faults to them, etc., so that they would not be infatuated with themselves. Abu Othman chose a third method, saying: "Both methods are good; each of them has its application depending on circumstances."

(To be continued.)[18]

ABDUL HÂDI

---

18 Editor's note: The article was not continued.

INTRODUCTION

"L'Islam et les religions anthropomorphiques" is in fact a reformulation of some of his observations in "Notes on Islam" where he explained Islam's unique antipathy to anthropomorphism and its subsequent aversion to idolatry and clergy.

It was especially appreciated by René Guénon who used it in his "Symbolism of the Cross".

Islam and Anthropomorphic Religions

La Gnose, No.5, May 1911

FOLLOWING SOME OBSERVATIONS conveyed to me regarding my previous articles, I felt obliged to make the subsequent declaration as a precaution against any possible misunderstandings.

Islam is not a religion that is based upon anthropomorphism. This is the reason for prohibiting the representation of God in any form, as any image of God is considered an idol. For Islam's mission is the abolishment of idolatry. The text of the Quran specifies this in numerous passages, especially in the sublime and venerated "Throne Verse", a passage which is well-known and thoroughly studied by the adepts of the Muslim Kabbalah. In it, it is clearly stated that nothing can bear any resemblance to God.

In correct religious Arabic, one may not simply say "The Lord" (*"ar-Rabb"*) without any apposition. Thus, one always says "The Lord" of someone, of something, of all, or of the All. Nowhere is "The Lord" proclaimed in an absolute sense. That would be the negation of all individual freedoms by imposing unto everyone the same aspect, or the same conception, of the Supreme Being.

Yet there exists, in practice, a certain anthropomorphism in Islam, but only as an indulgence, a provisional concession, due to the frailness of human comprehension. All ideas that are thought of with a certain intensity, ultimately become a "figure", and take on a human form – that of the thinker. It seems as if thought is poured into man much as molten metal is poured into the mold of the founder. The intensity of thought shall then fill man in his entirety, much like water fills a vase to the brim. It thus takes on the form of whatever contains and restricts it, that is, it becomes anthropomorphic.

The desire to relate everything to one's petty ego, one's distinct species or particularities, is no more than a fatal imperfection from which one can hardly escape. It is evident that the pretension of wanting to impose one's imperfections upon all of mankind, is indeed the height of despotism and heresy.

Yet, sentimentalism is the inability to distinguish Eternal Truth from the minor accidents of one's own exclusive and egotistic life.

Islam is the only religion in the world that can do without clergy or sacerdotal institutions of any form, as it firmly rests upon the basis of Tradition.

The clerical concept is evidently anti-Islamic, which is why priests of all robes and sects harbour a fierce loathing of Muslims. That these in fact respect Christian priests – in accordance with the strict command of the Quran – is of no consequence to them. Thus imagine: a belief that renders the entire [anthropomorphic] enterprise superfluous, or even noxious!

Two things necessitate the priest: the idol and the conventionalism of sentiments referred to as sentimentalism. There is moreover a close rapport between the two. They seem like the exoterism and esoterism of the same doctrine. Sentimentality is a kind of inner idolatry, in the same way as the idol is collective sentimentality in tangible form. Idol, priest and sentimentalism are thus the three aspects of all anthropomorphic religions. Yet Islam is not such a religion, neither by the letter, nor by the spirit. It loathes the idol, spurns the priest (except those of other religions), and shuns sentimentalism.

ABDUL HÂDI

*"Sentimentality is a kind
of inner idolatry, in the
same way as the idol is
collective sentimentality in
tangible form."*

"I make no claim of stating anything new.
What I say is old, truly old –
from such ancient times that all did forsake it."

L'Encyclopedie
Contemporaine Illustrée

1912-1913

INTRODUCTION

Upon returning to Paris from Sweden in mid-1912, Aguéli learnt that during his absence, René Guénon's La Gnose had unexpectedly closed due to financial difficulties. His friend Marie Huot thus found him a job as an art critic for the periodical "L'Encyclopedie Contemporaine Illustrée".

One of Aguéli's first tasks was to attend a large public exhibition of Cubist works – the "Salon de la Section d'Or". Aguéli, unlike any critic of the day, proceeded to explain the metaphysics of Cubism and its relation to the concept of "pure art", the alchemical art he had previously explained in "Pages dedicated to Mercury". In many ways the text is a summary of many of the thoughts he had already expressed in La Gnose, but presented in a more concise and accessible manner.

One of the major art critics of the day (and a good friend of Picasso), Guillaume Apollinaire, was so impressed by Aguéli's text that he suggested they collaborate in a series of art publications. Although in desperate need for money, Aguéli turned him down, disappointed that Apollinaire had been "cold" to his metaphysics whilst keen to "snap up" anything he had to say about art.

This translation is an abridged version of the original.

LA SECTION D'OR
THE EXHIBITION AT GALERIE LA BOÉTIE

L'Encyclopedie Contemporaine Illustrée
No. 659, 15 November 1912

IF THE MASTERS Picasso, Le Fauconnier and Van Dongen – the most important figures of contemporary art – had been able to participate in this year's *Salon de la Section d'Or*, it would have been an almost complete manifestation of all the novel currents of art. [...]

Cubism, conceived as a discipline, is in fact that which infallibly leads to the simple truth, that is to say, to the greatest possible exactitude rendered by the least possible means. This is the most rigorous of personal visions expressed in the briefest of ways. As Cubism, at least in my opinion, commences from the fundamental truth that the first subject to be painted in a painting is precisely space itself, and since the very portrait of a space – if I dare to express myself as such – cannot be expressed except by means of the exact proportions between distances, lines and luminosities – it thus follows that Cubism is, above all, the voluntary architecture of the clear or obscure masses of the void. We consequently see that Cubism, in its very principles, is nothing extraordinary except for its sheer audacity. It is nothing but the harshest method known today by which to study the exactitude of values and the preciseness of drawing. For the exactitude of values is indeed the fundamental law of all painting. [...]

For this pure art, which is not veiled by any sentimentalism *à la mode*, which makes no concessions to the aesthetic habits of the multitude, which is as devoid of any theatrical pretexts as it is of any "professional trickery" – such an art is veritably esoteric, that and none other, no matter what may be claimed by Monsieur Sar Péladan.[1]

Nothing is more from the occult sciences than the full transformation of rational and natural forms into Euclidian geometry. Is it not the highest kind of sorcery to express the most concrete

---

1 Editor's note: Sar Merodach Joséphin Péladan (1858-1918) was a Martinist novelist who gathered Symbolist painters, writers and musicians in his "Salon de la Rose + Croix" in Paris.

life in the most abstract of possible forms? In order to fully compre-hend that this is indeed a part of the Great Work which Eternity has imposed upon man, we merely have to look at how certain tropical cities, situated at the very nerve-centres of the world, well-known by tradition, that seemingly appear, when viewed from a certain height, as the synthesis of the landscape that surrounds them. Such a temple, such a sanctuary, is in turn the synthetic crown of the city it sanctifies. Or, allow us to, on the anthropomorphic plane, consider the manner by which such a Holy man, such a "Friend of God", has summed up his entire existence, his vast knowledge of the inner life, into a novel rhythm, having an occult sense that is beyond that of spoken words, something that is far richer and far more eloquent than the speech of any discourse.

Now, the exactitude of the rapport between anything that may stem from personal accentuations, especially between the landmarks chosen by the particular taste of each artist, is no more than the cre-ation of a personal rhythm, in other words, a novel rhythm. When this rhythm is directly expressed, you have before you a gesture of an art that is pure, cerebral and esoteric, which is neither ancient nor mod-ern, neither Eastern nor Western, neither wild nor civilised, but which is Art nevertheless, art that is forever young and invariable, having the ability to radiate in all eras, in all countries and in all climates. Once this rhythm wishes to manifest itself merely by way of a specific medium, be it cosmomorphic, anthropomorphic, social or otherwise – which are more or less impeding intermediaries – then you are in the presence of a hybrid art that is sentimental and exoteric.

As its taste depends on the visual trends of a certain era, region, race or climate, then one may indeed speak of concepts such as ancient art, modern art, etc. Futuristic painting failed to greatly inter-est Paris as everyone sensed that futurism could only touch upon this inferior form of art, which is sentimental art. In the realm of art, the proponents of the Past, Museum-lovers, Modernists and Futurists, are all sentimentalists.

In the case of pure art, the artist works for none but himself, seeking only to please himself. Yet, in the course of the work, he con-centrates himself, so as to ultimately become his higher I, his very Self, to the exclusion of all else, in complete solitude, above all in inner solitude, he thereby purifies himself of all foreign alloys, which are reminiscences of peoples or things, be they the atavisms of ethnicity, geography, climate or otherwise. [...]

These were the artists I found the most interesting: Juan Gris, Agero and Mlle. Laurencin. The first seems to be to almost personify the [Cubist] movement, although he is hardly amongst its founders. Having possessed a great skill that was based upon an adorable talent, in the ordinary sense of the word, which had earned him fame with all of its material consequences: he abandoned it all – routine, commissions, fortune – to follow the call of a nascent genius to the new, to something mysteriously personal and distinguished. I cannot help but to consider him an alchemist, seeking a novel conception of space – new, surprising, radiant. […] Mlle. Laurencin, her works shall one day come to be exhumed and gloriously compared to the fairest Manet and Constantin Guy. […] Glaizes, Metzinger and Picabia take up almost half of the exhibition. I would not say that they have yet found their definite formula, but they have indeed reached a certain stage of their evolution. […]

Abdul Hâdi

INTRODUCTION

In this article Aguéli once more explains his thoughts on sculpturing and architecture and draws parallels between art and literature. In many ways, this article is a continuation of "On Western Art".

On the Principles of Monuments and Sculptures

L'Encyclopedie Contemporaine Illustrée
No. 661, 31 January 1913

(Declaration: I make no claim of stating anything new.
What I say is old, truly old, from such ancient times
that all did forsake it.)

ON THE SOCIAL PLANE, an artist is anyone who loves his vocation and takes great pleasure in his craft, whatever it may be. By this, his craft is marked by a unique imprint that above all attests to the spontaneity of his mental state – as it informs us of his taste. Man, in his entirety, is comprised of his loves and repulsions, yet one may indeed alter one's opinions, even one's perceptions, whilst still remaining true to oneself. From the point of view of Tradition and esoterism, the artist is the man with a mental perspective, the man who possesses, so to say, a personal sun created expressly for himself and which gives rise to a world of its own. It is the overall perception of this particular world, which revolves around the artist as if around a pole, which we refer to as the mental perspective of the particular man. It may indeed have this solar or aerial perspective in common with other observers of nature – much as how common geometry is shared by everyone – yet, his mental perspective shall always remain his very own, this being the secret of his entire productivity. Just as all the worlds [across the universe] depend upon their particular suns, the world of each particular artist is also formed by his own particular sun, which allows him to perceive reality in an entirely novel way. Yet, this particular sun is by itself the result of an entirely new endeavour – bold and solitary – towards *vivid immobility*, an intense longing to experience the "sensation of Eternity". Those who so far have followed our dissertation shall without difficulty understand, that the essential efforts of an artist must focus on issuing a radiation that would be, in a certain manner, the external reflection of his personal sun. Having noted that in the aestheticism of the vivid immobility, the universal opposition is represented on one hand by Life and on the other hand by Immobility, we hence state that the radiance of a work of art must come to embrace these two opposing sides, so that it – by way of harmony and serenity – may meld all antithetical and incompatible elements that appear when studied on their own.

Life is character, boldness, tingling, details. Immobility is synthetic abstraction, discipline, restraint or rather discerning judgement, source of order, unity and domination. Life, with its inclination towards precision, the concrete and the positive, tends to the future; whilst immobility tends more to the past. The latter is a voluntary arrangement, whilst the former consists of more or less circumstantial bouts of pain or pleasure. Music expresses above all the element of life, whilst architecture is particularly affected by immobility. It is therefore evident that in all the manifestations of art, there exist mixtures of the principles of melody and structure. Music brings forth a certain sympathy for creation. Oftentimes it generates a love for things. Architecture, at least when authentic, never laughs. It may even project a kind of ferocity – which I regard as beneficial. It is always more or less imposing. The architecture that fails to convey the idea of a progressive aggrandisement, continuous and supernatural, should not be regarded as such. The more its imaginary or hallucinatory proportions surpass its metric or "real" dimensions – the more it is prone to beauty. This is the reason why architecture is the supernatural *par excellence*, as it must appear as being greater than nature itself, if it wishes to justify its very *raison dètre* as an art.

We no longer have any true architecture. When a building appears to be smaller than it is in "reality", then we instantly know that we are in the presence of a modern work, even if it has been slavishly replicated from an older model.

The Arabs, the people of simplicity by way of synthesis, who possess the perfect knowledge of principles and essentials, have most discerningly come to cultivate music and architecture, the primitive types of art. From the combination of these two "sources", all the others are sprung, and are distinguishable from each other only by the proportions of the mixture, and by the particular – yet always exterior – circumstances of their manifestation. Painting, for example, is an art form that is comprised of one-half architecture and one-half music. Its indicative means is two-dimensional space. That of sculpturing encompasses three-dimensional space. This is, furthermore, also comprised of architecture and music. One may say that it is a kind of spatial painting around which one may walk and in which the element of "immobility" is three times more prevalent than the element of "life". Yet, as the essential function of radiance is to be a unifying unity, it follows that a statue – which is sculptural work *par excellence* – must always emanate the exact same amount of radiance, irrespective of the point of view from which it is being observed.

The sculptor is, by consequence, obliged to align the emanated harmony by means of the most different forms (lines, volumes, shadows, etc.), a harmony that the eye shall necessarily conceive as a luminous unity. This may only be achieved by a very strong and perfectly detailed consciousness of its radiance and all that relates to it. The method he employs to achieve this is his particular secret. We may round off by establishing that a statue is, much like a panorama, the combination of numerous paintings. Yet what is the periphery of a panorama becomes the centre when it is a question of a statue.

The study of radiance could make us find the quantitative measure of genius that reigns over each work of art. We have indeed already indicated that of architecture. That of sculpture would be the luminosity it emanates. However, it is important to remember the presence of a "black light". It exists, it is known to the mystics – at least to those of the Muslim tradition – and we see it in art as a kind of depth that attracts us irresistibly. The pictorial intensity of a painting is determined by the nature of the optical (or visual) axes of the painting, in other words, by the accentuation of the planes, by the way the figures arise and detach themselves from the background. The quality of a literary work is determined by the number of times it may be reread with enthusiasm. A poem that may be read ten times over is thus ten times more beautiful than one that can only be read once. Furthermore, a piece of writing that can only be read once, is not literature, but mere journalism.

Abdul Hâdi

INTRODUCTION

This article was Aguéli's last publication before his departure to Egypt in late 1913 and his subsequent passing in Spain in 1917. He speaks of the religious tolerance of the early Roman Empire and of the man who very much like himself "fled not only museums and studios, but also galleries, churches, vaults, cells, chapels, streets, taverns, etc. in order to be alone with God". Aguéli also mentions the Ancient and Perennial Tradition as that which is "imprescriptible and forever young".

This translation is an abridged version of the original.

THE 29TH EXHIBITION
OF LE SALON DES INDEPENDANTES

L'Encyclopedie Contemporaine Illustrée,
No. 664-665, 25 May 2013 and 30 June 1913

[...] THE EXHIBITION MERELY EXPRESSES the best aspect of the ancient Roman religion, which was its universalism – the commendable wish to grant all, even the utterly penniless, some sunshine. The barbarians have not realised the magnitude of this gesture, although they to the greatest extent have reaped its benefits. What am I saying? It is rather that without it, they would not even have existed. [...]

[...] In truth, all the artistic currents of the last century go back to the landscape painting of the romanticists. The aspiration for novelty beyond all schools and dogmas is reflected in the man who fled not only museums and studios, but also galleries, churches, vaults, cells, chapels, streets, taverns, etc. in order to be alone with God. Mark well, that I here speak of the Good God and of the good painter – not of the god of cads and rascals. I speak of the God that is carried within anyone, who at any moment in his life has truly sensed the "sensation of eternity", and that which one perceives when one, detached from all things, lifts one's gaze towards the horizon, that which is furthermost, in the void. For it is not the dread of the void, which is the primary proponent of art, as claimed by Monsieur Maurice Denis, the "Christian" painter – or rather the "Neo-Christian" *par excellence*. It is in fact, on the contrary, the supreme love for the void and the naked, a love that translates into an irresistible attraction to an immensity brimming with light, and which may only be populated by figures of abstract clarity. [...]

There is indeed much talk of a return to Tradition – with a capital letter, if you please – yet no one makes the effort to explain what this truly means. One may even get the impression that it falls within the purview of occult sciences, an esoterism of sanctuaries, or a secret that has been preserved by some mystic potentate of the spiritual realm. In the statements and works of "Christian" or "Neo-Christian" painters, "Tradition" is no more than an empty label by which to peddle fake antiques. We think of it differently. We have a higher notion of Tradition, and we cannot conceive of a secret doctrine existing in visual arts.

According to us, it is the very "spacism" that allows the rediscovery of the Ancient Tradition, that which is imprescriptible and forever young. For it is the ultimate triumph of light over darkness by using the aestival, solar and divergent perspectives, that the different planes of space widen in all directions, much like the movement of an unfolding fan. What is commonly referred to as "the void", the great terror of Christian painters, becomes, so to say, the brain, the very nerve-centre of the painting, for crossed over by dynamic currents that are profoundly meditated on by the artist, this "void" is indeed contextualised by determinants, from mere figures to a drawing of an essentially mental quality.** Thus, mastery in art, and the state of grace in Dervishism, both share the same characteristic: the sky rent open.

It is interesting to note that in Europe, those who have been favoured by the vision of the rending skies are nearly always rebellious or refractory.

Our notion is hence that Tradition, that is "spacism", or the doctrine of the personal style, according to which perfect harmony is attained between Impressionism and Classicism, as well as between all this in rapport with one of these concepts, and which seems, at first glance, to be no more than a muddle of contradictions.

We have said that Impressionism is the crying of the I which indeterminately aspires towards the plenitude and order of the future. It is imperious and obeys nothing, for it is hungry – hungry for perfection. Classicism is the experience of all the generations that are no more. Whoso is merely an Impressionist, is no more than an interesting barbarian. Whoso is merely a [Classicist] stylist, is no more than a rodent of tombs. The former is the image of the revolt; the latter is that of obedience, nothing more. Yet it is the man who faithfully abides by the laws of nature or logic from the impressions of his Higher Self, who shows us the fair example of the true human vitality of all eras and of all nations. He is the *dandy* of the romantics, as well as the outlines of the Universal man of Dervishism.

Abdul Hâdi

"According to us, it is the very 'spacism' that allows the rediscovery of the Ancient Tradition, that which is imprescriptible and forever young."

"I tremble when the Honourable Shaykh speaks admiringly of the so-called "progress". Does he want the East to become as ugly and miserable as Europe?"

Miscellanea

INTRODUCTION

*"On Western Art" is a unique attempt by Aguéli to explain the eso-
terism of Western art to his fellow Muslims. It has an anti-modern-
ist overtone, especially when addressing the destruction of ancient
monuments.*

*The manuscript seems to have been written with the intention of
being translated into Arabic for the Egyptian periodical "al Moayed"
– although it is not known if it was ever published.*

ON WESTERN ART

THANKS TO THE WORKS OF EMINENT SAGES, be they Arabs or Europeans, those Europeans that are of goodwill and education may acquire understanding and taste for the beauty of Muslim civilisation, and of Arab nations. Yet, those Easterners who want to learn about the beauty of the West – for it does indeed exist in spite of present appearances – find themselves limited to the descriptions of exported scholars and those who know well how to gain wealth, but who are wholly inept in matters of art. Thus, it is often left to adventurers and money-dealers to explain our works. And without indicating anyone specific, we may state that here the students know more than their teachers. Although this subtle matter requires a pen more skilled than mine, I shall nevertheless take the risk to explain to my Arab friends the true art of the nations of the West. No man has ever trod upon this path and I hope that my lack of erudition shall be compensated by my profound admiration of beauty, both the Arab and the Muslim. I thus pray to Allah to bless my effort; I commence in His Holy Name for a better comprehension and explication of His name *al Lateef*.[1]

Let us begin by stating that painting is not an unholy attempt to create something better than the Creator, but it is merely a way to understand His works and find the Creator in creation, to perceive the unity, the harmony and the balance of the multiplicity of things and appearances. It is a kind of poetic art, where the lines and colours replace the words, much like poetry often is a painting and an evocation of images through words. Hence, a well-chosen expression corresponds to a bold drawing.

By the examples of Nabiga, Seha Chamfara, Hariri, etc., one may state that the pictorial sentiment of the Arabs was expressed through their poetry. I can mention such examples *ad infinitum*, but not wanting to abuse the hospitality of *al Moayed*[2] I shall only cite that which illustrates my thinking.

---

1 Editor's note: The Divine name *al Lateef* has several meanings. One is "the Gentle", "the Gracious". Another is "the Subtle", the One Who knows the innermost secrets of all things. Aguéli is most probably referring to the latter meaning.

2 Editor's note: "*al Moayed*" was an Egyptian periodical for which this article must have been intended.

In the case of painting, it is absolutely the same as poetry, that beautiful paintings are just as rare as true poetry, and what pleases one, may not please another. Taste in painting is as personal as taste in poetry. None are considered beautiful by all, there are always some that are not liked, except by a certain group or in a certain time, whilst others remain disputed. And furthermore, there are those that are recognised in the multitude, and there are some that are like the pearls of the sea; long hidden in the greatest of depths, only to then shine upon the crown of kings.

Like poetry, painting is a subtle means of mental communication. By it, one may fully convey a mental state. The paintings of the Italians of the Renaissance render the mentalities of this era far better than any historical account. The reason for this is that art shows us the taste of a man, of an era, or a country. Now, man manifests himself much more in his taste, by what he accepts and rejects, than in his thoughts or deeds. Primarily, as actions may be imitated or carried out at the suggestion of others, they may also express the thoughts of others, and thoughts are like birds fluttering hither and thither, whilst someone's taste and spontaneity is difficult to conceal. Taste attracts and revolts us, it stems from emotions, desire, and the love of each one of us. And taste does not change until the very soul of man has changed. Emotions still evoke thoughts and actions, and thus they are the centre of the inner life of man. Thus, taste reveals to us the secrets of desire, and it is through the conveying of tastes that desires are communicated, and thus also mentalities. Art, like poetry, is a language of the soul, far more subtle than the language that only conveys thoughts.

They form bonds of intimacy, friendship, admiration, and consolation; not only beyond the conditions of fortunes and races, but also beyond the greatest of distances, beyond regions, borders and centuries. Art is the true mirror of the mind, and he who knows how to read the subtle writings of a work of art or a poem, he possesses the key to [human] consciousness.

Art and poetry are the treasures of emotion and intellectual life. This is why all intelligent governments safeguard their museums and monuments, for these are the true treasures of the traditions of a race or a nation. The objects, even the most insignificant ones, that carry upon them the imprints of the life and mentality of other times, contain – in their very form – something of those times. Any man who attentively crafts an object could be said to have seals on his fingers that he prints upon his work, and that his work contains something of himself. And many centuries later, a connoisseur may read his efforts, his calmness, or anxieties, in [the form of] his creation. Thus, the souls of the ancestors, and their spirits, come to live on through the crafted objects they have left behind. Together, these [crafted] things form an atmosphere where their spirit is perpetuated.

Invaders and razing conquerors know this all too well. And their primary concern is always to destroy the special and national character of national or religious monuments, to impose upon the vanquished, not only their own mannerisms, but also their sentiments. Thus, they sever traditions and the link between past and present, and they become the absolute masters of the future, without having to fight for it.

By now, I presume that the reader has come to comprehend what a work of art is, and that he understands its importance. It is any manifestation of consciousness and its fixation of taste and emotion, by giving the emotion a form that may resist distances in time, in regions, or in races, without losing its ability to grow and blossom in the soul of a kindred spirit.

How many thousands of elite beings have not shed tears, hoped, sobbed, loved, or gained strength and courage from [the lines of] an Imru al Qais or a Chamfara, in spite of the fourteen centuries and many thousands [of miles] in distance. Now, a painting by Leonardo da Vinci or Rembrandt is an analogous case.

If you are not, by birth, of a poetic nature, no one can teach you to enjoy or comprehend poetry, even less how to produce it. One cannot learn to be an artist as one would learn to be a government clerk. Either one is an artist, or one is not. Furthermore, one cannot be taught to love art if one does not have a natural disposition towards it. I shall therefore be very brief when speaking of the different classes of art, and I shall leave it to the Ulama and the Shaykhs to issue rulings on the depiction of things from a religious point of view.

I find any art that merely renders creation in all its accidents and details, to be inferior and useless, if not dangerous. I consider the art that merely renders the impression without reproducing the objects causing the impression, to be art *par excellence*. I consider the art that renders the object without this impression to be a vain effort and its practice to be futile, if not harmful. But often it is an object that makes an impression, and to render the one, one must depict the other. So, I believe that one must strive for the greatest possible simplicity and only render the bare necessity to make the impression, and thus seek the unity and vitality of nature. And there is a [Prophetic] tradition that recommends us not to fully depict living things. This precept, properly understood, must be followed, in the very interest of art.

We consider commemorative art and the statues of men to be inferior and may lead to idolatry. Superior art is that which depicts the dreams and visions of those that are most fortunate.

Yet, the manner of perception always comprises more soul and emotion than the thing that is perceived. The man who is close to God does not perceive in the same manner nor the same things as the man who is far from Him. As a man rises in spirituality, his manner of perception changes, and so a painting exactly renders a manner of perception that indicates a mental station. If one day a [Sufi] Shaykh would begin to paint, the "*mourid*" ["disciple"] would merely have to contemplate his works to reach his [spiritual] station, or just about. And the contemplation of works of art is a true initiation. Also, in Europe, no one is considered to be educated ("*adib*"), unless he knows the masterpieces of the artists, at least those of the principal ones.

To conclude: Painting is a genre of poetry, that is qualifying. Inferior painting qualifies things. Superior painting qualifies a mental state and a station of consciousness. The painting that solely imitates things may be an unholy work. The painting that expresses a spiritual state – through a vision of things – guides the soul to novel states of consciousness and fortitude.

ABDUL HÂDI

"If one day a [Sufi] Shaykh
would begin to paint, the
'mourid' would merely have
to contemplate his works to
reach his [spiritual] station, or
just about. And the contemplation of works of art is a true
initiation."

INTRODUCTION

"Les Europées et Les Musulmans" is a handwritten manuscript that was unpublished in the lifetime of Ivan Aguéli. It is a response to a Muslim Shaykh by the name of "Abdul Haqh" who seems to have written an article in a French review propagating for Pan-Islamism and agitating against Europe. The exact date of Aguéli's writing is unknown, but judging from its contents, it was probably written sometime between 1910-1912.

The reader should be mindful of the historical context of the text, as it was written in a world when there was an ongoing struggle for democracy, universal suffrage, and human rights in the West, and a struggle against colonialism in the East.

Aguéli explicitly condemns modern science and the notion of "Progress"', whilst praising the "true democrats" of Italy, France and England who fight against social injustice. He states that mankind should be proud of "human rights" as not all the "progenies" of the French Revolution were "as degenerated as one might think". He warns the Shaykh of agitation against Europe as a whole and questions his praise of modernism.

Aguéli then presents his own view of a union between "elect" esoterists of Islam, Judaism and Christianity who together may bridge the divide between East and West.

He presents East and West as being in a kind of yin-yang relationship – as complementary opposites of "rest" and "toil" that "must understand each other". This is very similar to Guénon's later definition of East and West as "contemplation" and "action". Aguéli also warns about times to come, of how a rupture between East and West will bring about a war of "evil against evil", dragging the world into an "age of darkness".

At the very end he emphasises that the Muslim esoterist is in fact an ally of the liberal revolutionaries of Europe.

This translation is an abridged version of the original.

ON EUROPEANS AND MUSLIMS

WE HAVE READ IN *LA REVUE*, the open letter of *Shaykh Abdul Haqh* to Europe in the name of Pan-Islamism. It is of utmost interest, both as a document and a manifesto.

I can well understand the many grievances harboured by the Honourable Shaykh, particularly as I too share them with him. Yet, I merely wish to make the following remark to him: that there is a difference between *Europe* and *Europe*, and that the Europe which evokes such hatred in the East, is in no manner any less hated in the West.

If the Honourable Shaykh had been able to study the social movements of Europe, he would certainly not have referred to it with terms such as "moral disorder" and "febrile agitation". It is our duty to tell him that the French Revolution had many progenies, which are not all as degenerated as one might think. Official "Republicans" claim a heredity to which they have no right whatsoever, whilst the legitimate children [of the Revolution] always support struggles against obscurantism and tyranny. Thus, to attribute the crimes of reactionaries, be they disguised or not, to true democrats is absurd. It is as monstrous as if to punish him who has been thieved, for the actions of the thief.

The Honourable Shaykh is wrong to direct his hatred against all Europeans. In the free nations of Italy, France and England, true democrats are doing their utmost to at first hinder the policies of colonial expansion, and then, they always – in the name of justice – take the side of the indigenous victims of their own compatriots.

There are those who for the sake of this cause not only risk their careers and their fortunes, but also their lives.

In Europe, where there is neither religion, nor prayers, nor mosques, there is only one consolation. That is the ardour of the hearts of an elite haunted by a distant and somewhat obscure dream, fighting with an unmatched heroism against a society bolstered by infernal sciences and entirely based upon hatred. One may think that in the countries that have not yet been enlightened by Islam, there are those who are Muslims in silence, without knowing it. They fight and they die for an ideal. They know that their victory is not of this world. They do not have time to meditate upon other things, since they are fully absorbed by the struggle.

The Prophet of God has said: "The apotheosis ("*niemah*") of death is a man who dies for his rights." Yet, the men of whom we speak, die not for their own rights, but for the sake of wretches who do not know, who do not dare, and who accept their sacrifice without the slightest gratitude. [...]

The European, how do you want him to pray, he who has never heard the call of the *muezzin*? In his cold country, sad and cursed by the abandonment of God, he has lost his hieratic sense. Therefore, ritual and prayer remain closed to him. The absence of sacred architecture, décor and colour make profound and religious emotions difficult, as well as perceptions of the eternal and fixed world. In spite of this, it is rather rare to find a European who is hostile to the Muslims for any other reason than ignorance. He wants to learn from elsewhere, but a sound education is difficult to obtain when it comes to the East.

Know then that there are highly powerful parties, in whose vital interest it is that East and West should hate each other. They only exist due to this loathing, and the day that East and West truly get to know each other, the powers of darkness shall be vanquished.

Many Europeans have converted to Islam. The educated, independent European almost always loves the East, not only by fashion, but by taste. If Muslims had been familiar with the spirit of the Europeans, there would have been conversions in droves. I have known Europeans who have been moved by the recitation of the Sublime Quran, by the contemplation of beautiful and ancient mosques, and by processions and religious gatherings. A new convert, who was insidiously asked why he had become a Muslim, replied: "For I love minarets more than factory chimneys, and I prefer the turban to the black hat".[1]

The literary beauty of the Quran is a proof of its celestial origin. The beauty in architecture, décor and life is not only the work of a faith that is intense and pure, but it is also the foremost weapon and safeguard of that very faith.

---

1 Editor's note: In the original manuscript, the last sentence "*and I prefer the turban to the black hat.*" was crossed over by Aguéli, but we kept it as it was a fitting complement to the entire sentence.

And so, the most pressing task of fools and foes is to destroy the sources of the transcendent sensations that arise from the ancient monuments, the arts and the traditions of dress and gestures, and which help us revert to a mental state of more glorious times. I tremble when the Honourable Shaykh speaks admiringly of the so-called "progress". Does he want the East to become as ugly and miserable as Europe?

Herein lies the gist of European progress: Primarily, it is the art of making devices of ruin, cannons, machine guns, etc., that is to say, the art of slaughter. Furthermore, it is the art of hoarding money, and that by a fiscal system, according to which the citizen cannot eat, nor drink, nor clothe himself without paying a tax that ultimately turns exorbitant. It is the art by which to starve and to thieve.

As for Human Rights, of which the world should be proud, they are only achieved in Europe by terrible upheavals in society as a whole. Had there been no revolutionaries, the Christian nations would have been nothing but a mass of inebriated slaves, always ready to inundate the East with blood and gore at the slightest whim of some king or priest. What a pity that we cannot in the aftermath of a revolution echo the great French poet, Victor Hugo: "What makes us strong is that we can unleash the people upon any King who unleashes his army. A revolution shall fight for us wherever we want."

For the most part, their industrial and technical discoveries are only needed at home. They must [use them to] withstand a harsh, sad, and inhospitable climate, which for that matter much resembles themselves. As for the rest, there is a give and take. One of their greatest writers Villiers de l'Isle Adam has said: "... that the primary boon, for which we are positively indebted to science, is to have placed the simple, essential and "natural" things of life, *out of the reach of the poor.*"

Their famous medical science consists mainly of hygiene. Yet, the teachers of hygiene were not physicians, but their clients, the sick and the deceased. Practical medicine has not made any real progress for more than fifty years, thanks to the development of what they refer to as "pure science". Its very name is a profanation for it contains neither truth, nor purity. It is the most bizarre aberration of the human spirit since the fall of *Iblis*. It would possibly be ridiculous had it not been for the death of its victims. At present, it is sinister. What could be more abominable than all these minor natural, biological, physiological religions, etc., that pass us by, one after another? For a number of months or a number of years they strew about them death and suffering. They poison the sustenance of the body, the sustenance of the soul and the remedy of the sick, then they disappear. The false prophet remains nonetheless, revered as a demi-god, and almost always a millionaire.

Muslims may take from European sciences everything that concerns numbers, iron, earth, navigation, that is to say: mathematical sciences, physics, inorganic chemistry, and metallurgy. That is all it takes for defence and prosperity. Modern science is a secular science, and it must not, *under any pretext*, come to touch upon life itself, nor its necessities. [...]

I permit myself to differ with the Honourable Shaykh regarding the religion of the Europeans. Their sense of religion in no way resembles that of the Muslims. Amongst Europeans, religion is only a Sunday-concern, a pose, or colonial policy. The Germans also have a certain fear of the unknown and of death. Their theological discourses are more games of reasoning than a [true] study of religion.

Islam, on the other hand, penetrates all of life. It is norm and synthesis, being both the summary of traditions and a guide of conduct and attitude – at the very least it compels one to become and to aspire towards one's destiny. It is both ardent patriotism and resolute universalism. It has placed the homeland in the heart of man, which makes him feel at home everywhere. It is the only thing upon earth that is stronger than atavisms and heredities. I have seen Indians, born as Buddhists or Hindus, who after a few years of being Muslim come to change their posture and walk. All Muslims recognise themselves in a special way.

Now, compare this extraordinary vitality of Islam with Catholicism. Having been more Semitic and Eastern, it once bestowed on Europe almost the same homogeneity as that of Islam. Yet, with the pagan element having prevailed, it now produces nothing but atheists, vivisectionists or Satanists. No longer is it the bulwark against the inherent idolatry and materialism of the non-Semitic races it once was. No longer Semitic, Catholicism is debilitated, for Semitism is always vitality.

Islam, on the other hand, is the very essence of the Semitic idea. It has the simplest and most universal of formulae. Therefore, the *abasement of the Arabs corresponds to the abasement of Islam.*

This is why the Prophet of God recommended the study of Arabic calligraphy which is an inexhaustible source of emotion and Semitic art. This is also why the Arabs were placed at *the centre* of the other peoples, to serve as a unifying factor.

European and Christian are in no manner synonymous. Most Europeans are totally indifferent to matters of religion, and if the missionaries had been of good faith, they would have stayed at home to convert their own compatriots. We have seen how amongst religious Europeans, religion is not the same as it is with us.

Now let us speak of those Europeans who reflect upon their religion. There are thousands who consider the doctrine of the Trinity to be a metaphysical formula of action in general, roughly meaning: will, knowledge, power – and is unrelated to any kind of polytheism.

The cult of the Crucifixion requires a longer explanation. Ancient Europe was occupied by essentially ferocious races, completely closed to any sense of mercy. God, the Most High, whose ways are mysterious, accorded them a religion that softens their hearts, that is, the cult of unjust suffering and the tormented innocent. Being at their mercy, the weak or defeated were still shrouded by a Divine ray. It was a way to block the raised mace.

For the greatest faults, the greatest remedies.

Amongst Muslim nations, kindness and leniency are innate, and their application is spontaneous. They can be maintained by the most basic precepts of civility. Amongst Christian nations, it was necessary to make it into the most important religious dogma, or no one would have thought of it.

I believe to have demonstrated that religious differences – when there indeed is religion – between elect Muslims and Europeans do not necessarily constitute hostility. A difference in rituals may be an obstacle to intimacy, but not to an alliance in matters of principles where one is in agreement. Now, the three great Semitic religions – Islam, Christianity and Judaism – share a common basis: The good united in the Sublime, which is the True Good.

Christian mysticism is at every instant matched by Muslim spirituality. Why then should the good Muslim hate the good Christian, especially when they both face a common foe?

West is toil, East is rest. The one cannot be without the other and both are indispensable. They must understand each other. They unite in the solemn moments of history. The union of their good brings about an age of light, just as the union of their evils brings about an age of darkness. (To be understood as "*Hells*").

My words speak of peace between the good and the good, no matter from what side. They also speak of [a possible] war, not merely between good and evil, but between evil and evil.

The Muslim who reposes in the true contemplation of the Eternal and the Infinite – a state of mind which in one way or another always implicates the [Greater] Holy Effort [for one's inner soul] – cannot be the adversary of the European who in one way or another strives and fights for the ideals of liberty and justice.

I have spoken,

ABDUL HÂDI

"For I love minarets
more than factory chimneys,
and I prefer the turban
to the black hat."

INTRODUCTION

"Al Akbariyyah" was founded in Cairo at an unknown date and later "realised" in Paris on Thursday night, 22 June 1911. On the same night, Ivan Aguéli also received René Guénon into Islam and gave him the name "Abdul Wahid", the "Servant of the One".

Al Akbariyyah was meant to be a semi-official esoterist society that promoted the universalist teachings of Ibn Arabi in the West. It was most probably encouraged by Shaykh Abd ar-Rahman Elish in Cairo, who may have regarded it as a continuation of Emir Abd al-Qader's attempts to reach out to Western esoterists in the 1870s. Shaykh Elish and the Emir had been close friends during their exiles in Damascus, where they together had studied the teachings of Ibn Arabi.

Aguéli left for Sweden only a week after the founding of Al Akbariyyah and no one knows what became of it. Most probably Aguéli's absence and the closure of La Gnose in February 1912 led to the scattering of the remaining members, of whom only René Guénon later reasserted his Islam in public.

STATUTES OF
AL AKBARIYYAH

AL AKBARIYYAH IS A SOCIETY for the scientific study of the life and works of Mohyeddin Ibn Arabi. It is international, standing above all issues relating to race, castes, homelands, and national rivalries.

It was conceived, in Cairo in the year _____ [1] but could only be realised in Paris, on 22 June 1911 (Thursday night) which corresponds to the 26th of *Jumada al-Thani,* 1329 H.

Its aim is to make known to the civilised world ("civilisation" in the common sense) in East and West, the life and works of Shaykh Mohyeddin Ibn Arabi. This shall be done, not only through editions of his works but also through translations, philosophical and rational commentaries on his writings and by the founding of centres of Mohyeddinian studies, libraries, periodicals and study centres. It shall not only strive to explain the doctrine of the Master, but also to determine its position *vis-a-vis* the different doctrines or philosophies of all nations. It shall bring together the elite of all races and languages in an intellectual community which on one side touches the world of tradition and on the other the universal movement of our days.

It shall be realised depending on the circumstances. The work of the exterior shall always be formulated by one or more publications, polyglot if possible, which at the same time shall serve as an exterior platform for the different members.

Whilst awaiting a publisher of its own, it accepts with gratitude the hospitality generously offered to it by the Parisian journal "La Gnose". The languages used shall primarily be European. French, followed by English, Italian or Spanish, Arabic, and Chinese. Later on, one may also use: Turkish, Sanskrit, Hindi, Tamil, Persian and Malay.

It shall seek to construct a mosque in Paris which under its authority shall serve as a centre for reunions, studies, and spiritual retreats at suitable venues.

---

1 Editor's note: The year was left blank by Aguéli.

Each member should:

1. Formally recognise the unity of the Supreme Being.
2. The Prophetic mission of Mohammed.
3. Express affinity for the Shaykhul Akbar Mohyeddin Ibn Arabi and a desire to study his works in order to develop esoterically and commit to develop to the limits of his possibility.
4. One may not opt-out of giving one's word of honour not to be influenced by any clergy that is Christian, Jewish, Magian, Buddhist or pagan.

~~Thus it follows that an Akbarite may not be a Christian Protestant, Roman Catholic, Orthodox Catholic, Coptic, Nestorian, Jacobite, Joannite etc.. That he may neither be Jewish, nor fire-worshipper, nor Buddhist, nor idolater, [ineligible], nor an individualistic free-thinker, a freemason, etc..~~ [2]

Thus, an Akbarite may belong to any school of esoterism* (*Due to "*at Tawhidu Wâhidun*"). Yet on the other hand he may not belong to any other exoterism than that of Islam.** (** Since Mohyeddin faithfully followed the Prophetic tradition, which is incomprehensible to non-Muslims).

Apart from the four oaths made upon entering the society, there is only the payment of the dues which may vary according to personal circumstances. Inability to pay the contribution does not of itself serve as grounds for exclusion. Unwillingness to pay only results in the loss of the rights to benefits and materials of the association, whilst the violation of one of the four oaths is considered a betrayal.

§ The solidarity amongst the members is merely of an intellectual kind and limited by the rules of the statutes. A member's attitude in the world shall only concern the world. Apart from the common interest in their subject of study, a member has no further rights over another member, except for what is due by the Sharia, and no more. Apart from the formal obligations of the statutes, the Sharia is also the ultimate rule in the social interactions between different members.

---

2 Editor's note: Aguéli's cross-over, replaced by the paragraph immediately below.

Since one never knows what direction Akbarite studies may take, the statutes are bound to be negative, apart from purely administrative matters.

§ It shall never seek power, be it political, financial or administrative. It will only take from the world what is enough to defend itself from it.

§ Detachment from all kinds of politics, be they foreign, domestic, or international. Humanitarianism shall only be taken into account if it is part of a tradition. It is equally detached from any colonial questions and from conflicts of material interest between indigenous peoples and the Europeans. Yet it shall not be indifferent to that which is of a purely Islamic interest, defined as such by the Sharia. Then, and only then, does it take the side that is inevitably pro-Islamic.

§ Whilst accomplishing the aims of its exterior work, it avoids placing any kind of restriction on the personal freedoms of the members.

§ Avoid all contacts with various exoteric clergy. An Akbarite who has dealings with a priest or member of the clergy may only do so at his own personal behest. The relations of the society with various groups that are intellectual, social, religious, humanitarian or other will be exposed by the press, by way of criticism, controversies or correspondences.

§ There is no harm in the different members of the society forming groups of their own within the society, as long as they do not intend to abolish the *raison d'être* of the society, that is to say, to violate the 4 oaths.

ADMINISTRATION

1. Contributions are made by subscribing to periodicals and the subscriptions from the specialised bookstore.
2. The Supreme Council shall direct the society. It is composed at most of 12 members, six of whom are European by birth. These are appointed by the founding members.

The present founding members are: signatures

They have elected *M. Champrenaud* as General Manager.

[RECOMMENDED READING]

El Bokhari, Les Traditions
Zohar, Tr. Pauly, Talmud, Pauly
Yiking, Les 4 livres; Recomp. et peines,
Tao-te king; De Harlez, Textes Taoïstes.
Dabry de Thiersant; L'Islamisme en Chine
Budge; Le livre des morts.
Norberg, Liber Adami
Les évangiles apocryphes
Le livre de Hénoch
Piatis Sophia, Amé Lineaus. Le gnost. Egypte
Schwab L'angelologie avec suppl.
Bhagavad gita, Kalevala, Edda
Legendes de iles de la mer du Sud
Fabre d'Olivet
Swedenborg, Arcanes
St Martin
Wronski
Stan de Guaita
Matgioi
Warrain

INTRODUCTION

The following text is a transcript of a note found amongst the letters and notes of Ivan Aguéli. It is – to our knowledge – the only text where Aguéli expresses himself directly in English.

The note is dated 1 November 1911, when he was residing in Stockholm and the recipient is unknown. It was included in this anthology merely as a historical curiosity – a precious one, nevertheless.

Note in English

Stockholm I/XI 1911

Dear Sir!

I take the great liberty to knock at Your door before appointed time. Would it be possible to see You a short moment or after tomorrow b.n.

Expecting Your precious reply
I am your most obedient servant
Aguéli

Central Post – restante
S.W.

J'ai parlé.
Abdul Hâdi

["I have spoken"]

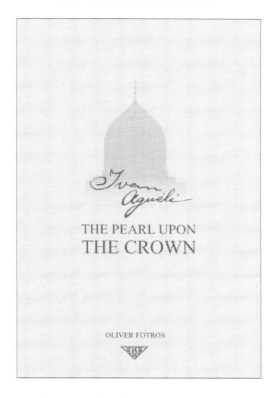

THE PEARL UPON
THE CROWN

OLIVER FOTROS

In "Ivan Aguéli - the Pearl upon the Crown"
Oliver Fotros explores the profound influence
of Ivan Aguéli on the works and ideas of the
French scholar René Guénon.

By examining Aguéli's original articles and
letters in French, Swedish and Arabic, Fotros
proceeds to decipher the texts of Guénon -
which uncovers facts that have been well con-
cealed for over a century. The result offers a new
perspective on one of France's greatest intellec-
tuals and a fascinating account of friendship,
intrigue, and ambition.

ISBN: 978-91-519-8508-4

Printed in Great Britain
by Amazon

64355036R00085